Arts & International Affairs

Also from Westphalia Press
westphaliapress.org

ARTS & INTERNATIONAL AFFAIRS JOURNAL

Volume 5, Issue 1 • Summer 2020

J.P. Singh, editor

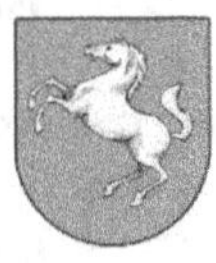

Westphalia Press

An imprint of Policy Studies Organization

ARTS & INTERNATIONAL AFFAIRS
VOLUME 5, ISSUE 1 • SUMMER 2020

Westphalia Press
An imprint of Policy Studies Organization
1527 New Hampshire Ave., NW
Washington, D.C. 20036
info@ipsonet.org

ISBN: 978-1-941755-19-8

Cover and interior design by Jeffrey Barnes
jbarnesbook.design

Daniel Gutierrez-Sandoval, Executive Director
PSO and Westphalia Press

Updated material and comments on this edition
can be found at the Westphalia Press website:
www.westphaliapress.org

DEMOCRATIZING ARTS

Our Longform articles are double-blind peer reviewed. The Brushstrokes and
Multimodal articles undergo an extensive in-house editorial process.

EDITORIAL:
DEMOCRATIZING THE ARTS AND THE ARTS SECTOR

RAPHAELA HENZE

Arts and cultural managers working in the fine and performing arts and heritage engage with creative and aesthetic expressions—arts and cultural objects, exhibitions and performances—that are inherently reflective of broader social as well as personal cultural ideas, knowledge, and values.

Building an understanding of their work will help us understand the contribution of the arts and its agents as to how historical, institutional and social assumptions about interculturalism, cultural diversity, and cultural inclusion become established and challenged in the social world. We consider this understanding essential when addressing the anxieties that globalization and an increasing populism bring to the arts and cultural sector.

In directing, administering, and mediating artistic and cultural expressions, arts and cultural managers work at the interface of production and consumption. In doing so, they contribute to how the terms and conditions for intercultural exchange are set both at home and abroad. The intercultural experiences or exchanges they help create may foster the acknowledgement, appreciation, and valuing of alternative perspectives and perceptions of the world or, conversely, promote and reinforce stereotypes and inequitable relationships between individuals, communities, institutions, and even nations.

Since its foundation in 2016, the international and interdisciplinary Network 'Brokering Intercultural Exchange' (www.managingculture.net) brings researchers together with arts and cultural practitioners and policymakers. Over the last couple of years, the Arts & Humanities Research Council funded network succeeded in bringing together around 250 people in different places for small seminars on specific topics. Participants from more than 40 countries have been joining the seminars, two Winter Schools—specifically targeting master and Ph.D. students—as well as the Annual Gathering. We aim to build an understanding of the relationship of arts and cultural management practice and education to intercultural exchange—interaction between communities, institutions, and /or nations with different 'values' and perspectives and individuals with different social, economic, and religious backgrounds. While we have mainly been focusing on "ethnically-marked cultural difference associated with the international movement of peoples and, within national territories", (Bennett 2001: 17), we acknowledge that intercultural/transcultural exchange happens across many groups and communities and involves concerns such as sexuality, gender, religion, class, and disability.

The texts presented in this special issue represent some of the ideas and concerns raised during the network's Annual Gathering entitled 'Democratizing the arts and the arts sector that took place in May 2019 at Heilbronn University in Germany. We considered ourselves lucky and privileged to have had amazing participants from around 20 countries and all continents. We are aware that being able to convene with colleagues from African countries for instance is unfortunately and for a variety of reasons—that urgently need to be addressed—by far a matter of course. However, we are also aware that an invitation to debate issues of exclusion and (in)equality does not in and of itself redraw or rebalance lines of power (Durrer/Henze 2018: 3).

A central concern that had been raised not only during the Annual Gathering's discourses but throughout the entire work of the network, was whether democracy can be managed through a discourse of diversity (Taylor Brown et al. 2019; Cuyler 2015; Dubois 2016; Purwar 2014: 1; Schonfeld/Sweeny 2016). How can democratization of the sector be achieved by avoiding what some authors even call a "Benetton model of diversity" in which diversity becomes an aesthetic style or an opportunity to give organisations a better image (Ahmed 2012: 53) but does nothing to address the deep causes of exclusion and power imbalances in the arts (Canas 2017)?

Gargi Shindé's text about her work for Chamber Music America (www.chamber-music. org) and her referral to both unintended bias as well as a history of blatant racism and active discrimination in orchestras gives compelling insights. That minorities, who created music, which has than become a national cultural commodity, despite questionable authenticity, did and do not actually participate in its commercial success particularly but not exclusively in the USA, is as much discussed in post-colonial theory as is the role of ideology in the production of pop music (George 2005). Gargi's work for grant equality is therefore unfortunately as important as hopefully superfluous someday soon.

Mihai Florea's timely take on the funding policy of the Arts Council England, that has to be understood as exemplary for other funding bodies as well, fits in this context. Mihai, co-founder of Nu Nu theatre, critically examines the funder's requirements when it comes to e.g. diversity and participation—often referred to by practitioners as ticking boxes. However, it is not only the funding policy that is in the focus of this text but also the 'role' artists have to play in these 'publicly funded' contexts. We need more bold texts like this and courageous authors like Mihai. It is unfortunately still a dicey thing to criticize a funder when you depend on their support. However, it will only be possible to improve funding strategies for the better when funders allow critical but constructive feedback and ideas on aspects of sustainability and measurement—unfortunately not many (neither practitioners nor researchers) dare to provide it (Henze 2017: 64).

Jason Vitorillo also asks questions concerning budget allocation and cultural governance referring to his native Philippines. He critically examines the policy of the National Committee for Culture and the Arts. The allocation of support goes to a few and not necessarily to the ones that seem to have the highest impact on society despite all difficulties to measure this.

Alex Tam, co-founder of Play Dot, refers to another important aspect raised during the Annual Gathering: democratizing the arts practice in order to involve more and diverse people in the artistic process and while doing so gaining more societal as well as social relevance (Henze 2017). What Alex as practitioner tries to achieve through public practice and activities—that particularly but not exclusively involve children—is even more relevant given the fact that he is working in Hong Kong. His idea of creating a 'safe space' has become a new and urgent notion throughout the last months of political turmoil.

Zainab Mussa Shallangwa is equally referring to societal relevance. In contrast to Alex, who co-founded a new, private organisation, Zainab is referring to museums in Borneo State, Nigeria. This text is central because it explains the educational as well as societal functions of an institution that has a colonial legacy. Some of the challenges Zainab is reporting, like a lack of financial resources and declining understanding of the social relevance in the political realm, sound vaguely familiar to "Western" curators but running a museum close to a Boko Haram headquarter, adds complexities most might be unfamiliar with.

Qinhan Chen's contribution on intercultural learning of musicians fits well into the network's research questions that centre on the role of intercultural education, which I consider underrepresented in academic discourses. My own contribution on Empowerment and Digitization hints in the same direction. I explain what I consider is missing in arts and cultural management education in order to empower aspiring cultural managers to set agenda instead of merely reacting to unforeseen challenges.

Finally yet importantly, I am happy to have Khaled Barakeh as a contributor to this special volume. An artists and cultural activist whom I admire for a long time. Khaled has founded CoCulture (https://coculture.de) in 2017 as a response to the challenges faced by displaced cultural producers in the Middle East, Europe and beyond. His work will speak for itself.

I would also like to thank J.P. Singh, who has been a fierce supporter of the Brokering Intercultural Exchange Network from the very start, for the opportunity to edit this special volume. It is a great pleasure and an honour. I am deeply convinced that we need more of these high-quality open source publications in order to reach out to as many colleagues in academia and practice as possible. I also thank all the authors, who have gathered last year at Heilbronn University and will hopefully return to this year's Annual Gathering in November, for their valuable and insightful contributions. I have learned a lot working with you.

LITERATURE

Ahmed, Sara. (2012) *On Being Included. Racism and Diversity in Institutional Life*, Duke University Press, Durham.

Bennett, Tony. (2001) Differing diversities. Cultural policy and cultural diversity. Strasbourg Cedex: Council of Europe Publishing.

Brown, Marion T. et al. (2019) *Moves Towards Equity: Perspectives from Arts Leaders of Color.* https://static1.squarespace.com/static/582a42725016e1e43d93cff2/t/5d8 02fbb84ad963f782ebfed/1568681918026/Moves+Towards+Equity+-+Final.pdf (Accessed 18 January 2020).

Canas, Tania. (2017) *Diversity is a white word,* http://www.artshub.com.au/education/ news-article/opinions-and-analysis/professional-development/tania-canas/diver sity-is-a-white-word-252910 (Accessed 19 February 2017).

Cuyler, Antonio. (2015) *An Exploratory Study of Demographic Diversity in the Arts Management Workforce,* Published in: GIA Reader, Vol 26, No 3 (Fall 2015).

Dubois, Vincent. (2016) *Culture as a Vocation. Sociology of career choices in cultural management.* New York: Routledge.

Durrer, Victoria/Henze, Raphaela. (2018) *Leaving comfort zones.* In Arts Management Quarterly, Leaving comfort zones. Cultural Inequalities, No. 129, June 2018, 3.

George, Nelson. (2005) *hiphopamerica.* New York: Penguin Group.

Henze, Raphaela. (2017) *Introduction to International Arts Management.* Wiesbaden: Springer

Purwar, Nirmal. (2004) *Space Invaders: Race, Gender, and Bodies out of Place.* Oxford: Berg Publishers.

Schonfeld, Roger C./ Sweeny, Liam. (2016) *Diversity in the New York City.* Department of Cultural Affairs Community http://www.sr.ithaka.org/publications/diver sity-in-the-new-york-city-department-of-cultural-affairs-community/ (Accessed 5 December 2016).

EQUITABLE GRANTMAKING IN PRACTICE: ARTISTS AS THE GENESIS OF AN INCLUSIVE CREATIVE ECOLOGY

GARGI SHINDÉ
Chamber Music America

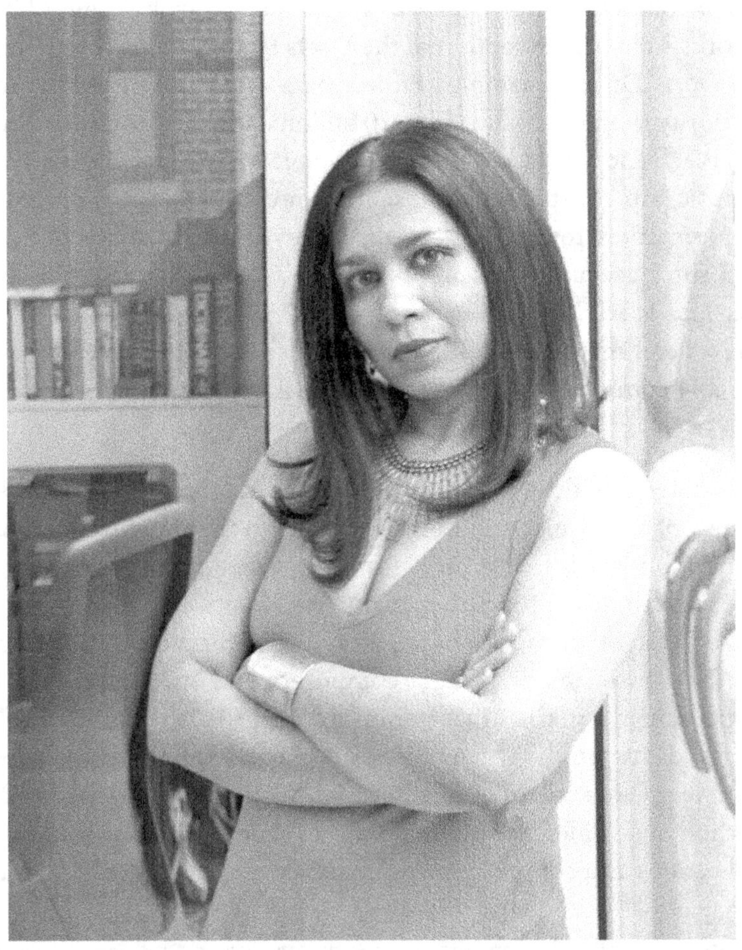

Gargi Shindé is Program Director for Jazz at Chamber Music America. She leads three programs distributing over $3.1 million in support for creation, presentation, touring, and ensemble development in the field of jazz. She recently launched CMA's Performance Plus program, supporting women bandleaders by creating apprenticeship opportunities with veteran jazz icons. She is a contributor to "RE-Tool: Racial Equity in the Panel Process," a resource to achieve racial equity in the grants review and selection process of artists and arts organizations. Gargi has over a decade of experience in arts education, program curation, and artist development. She has lectured on

classical Indian performance history and the aesthetics of improvisation at conferences in the United Kingdom, Spain, Canada, and the United States. Gargi is a classically trained sitarist and composer, whose collaborations bridge Indian classical music and the traditions of jazz.

The focus of my work as Program Director for Jazz at Chamber Music America (CMA)[1] involves tackling systems of absencing, which beleaguer US institutional frameworks. With the exception of the Doris Duke Charitable Foundation, which launched the Doris Duke Ensembles Project, jazz –America's heritage art form—is a diminished priority in an approximately $20 billion national arts philanthropy portfolio. Furthermore, Black and Latinx composers and performers, the originators and innovators of this music, are conspicuously absent from commissioning programs and grant support for presentation, touring, and audience development, especially the cultivation of Black and Latinx jazz audiences across the US. CMA's own flagship commissioning program, *New Jazz Works,* which awards up to $37,000 to a single jazz composer-bandleader, has never commissioned a Latina composer in its twenty-two year history. Of the program's 234 commissioned works, less than 3 percent are created by Black female composers.

Faced with an untenable future, CMA's Board of Directors began discussing issues of diversity, inclusion, and equity and how they relate to the organization's overall impact in the small ensemble music field. Our *Statement of Commitment,* adopted in 2017 states, "CMA believes that there is a fundamental difference between inviting ALAANA[2] communities into a Western European-based structure and revising the structure itself to include ALAANA musicians, presenters, composers, and others in the field to fully benefit as active participants in the organization" (CMA 2017). Equipped with only anecdotal or unverified data on the racial composition of its membership, grant applicants,[3] panelists, grant recipients, board of directors, leadership and staff, we needed to rapidly activate a method of self-identification in order to examine the organization's programs, services, publications and communication channels to fully understand the people who

---

1   CMA is a national membership organization for the creators, practitioners, presenters, educators and advocates of small ensemble music. It supports the national music community of over 6,000, mainly from the fields of classical, contemporary, jazz and new music, providing access to resources and benefits, such as professional development seminars, publications, grants and awards, and media tool kits, and through its annual National Conference, the opportunity to connect with a network of musicians, presenters, managers, other small ensemble music professionals, and institutional stakeholders across the country.

2   Demographic data collection acronym adopted by CMA (African/Latinx/Asian/Arab/Native-American).

3   CMA, since 1999, has implemented and administered the Doris Duke Ensembles Project. In addition to *New Jazz Works,* CMA administers five grant programs for the creation and presentation of jazz and classical music, and ensemble development.

create, perform, and present these music traditions. The jazz program became the pivotal benchmark for us to gauge progress.

Jazz presents a unique sociological lineage. Its genealogy is inextricably linked with systems of oppression, and the experience of marginalization and exclusion. The infinite and awesome original repertoire created by Black and Latinx artists in this music, to capture Homi Bhabha, remains a persistent intervention "in those ideological discourses of modernity that attempt to give a "hegemonic 'normality' to the uneven development and the differential, often disadvantaged, histories of nations, races, communities, peoples." Yet its institutional appropriation by the academy, its absorption into Western European classical aesthetics, jazz criticism, and patronage have virtually written out its multicultural, syncretic encounters in aesthetic development—the spirituality of jazz as it were. Apart from the commodification of yoga perhaps, it would be hard to come up with an example of a practice so completely untethered from its cultural roots.

So, how would CMA go about instilling inclusivity in the funding landscape when grants selection processes were established through the framework of the Western European classical conservatory model of excellence? How would we assess the very notion of *excellence*? Whose practice determines *innovation* in this music? What is the value of receiving a substantial commission, the privilege of unencumbered creativity in a largely unregulated performance industry? With the conservatory divide in jazz pedagogy, which artist groups historically have received the information, the know-how to enter the institutional systems of arts funding, the privilege to receive the financial endorsement, and the eventual entry into the greater mainstream cultural narrative? Interrogating equity thus became the starting point.

In search for answers, I was guided by alternative modes of documenting jazz. Photographs of iconic artists as Miles Davis, Thelonious Monk, and Bud Powell brutally beaten by police just moments after a performance or pivotal studio session, force us to confront the circumstances of creative production and artistic realization. In the zeitgeist of the Black Lives Matter movement, several contemporary and millennial black jazz artists including Terence Blanchard (*Breathless*), Greg Lewis (*The Breathe Suite*), Samora Pinderhughes (*The Transformations Suite, The Healing Project*) and Christian Scott (*K.K.P.D/ Ku Klux Police Department*) remind us that for Black jazz artists and audiences, artistic creation and reception does not merely begin and end at its aesthetic parameters. To evoke Bhabha again, "it forces us to confront the concept of culture beyond the canonization of the "idea" of aesthetics, to engage with culture ... produced in the act of social survival." Artists are themselves dynamic, living archives rarely factored into mainstream narratives of jazz. Pianist Don Pullen and drummer Andrew Cyrille, two of jazz's most iconic innovators, as young artists, performed for the domestic staff of the mansions of East Hampton, NY, which were comprised entirely of black women at the time, until those bars closed. Where does the legitimacy of excellence formed by an authentic and robust audience of Black female, domestic workers factor into the juggernaut of art music criticism and tastemaking?

The metaphor expanded includes many untold or interrupted stories, such as New Orleans and Puerto Rico: records, tools, instruments, compositions, and entire oral histories lost in displacement and environmental devastation; entire creative habitats undone; audiences wiped out. Under what circumstances are these master artists producing *excellence*, while simultaneously finding themselves absent from the larger momentum shaping the American cultural landscape? The possibility then for CMA to commission iconic artists, such as Andrew Cyrille, Wayne Shorter, David Murray, Nicole Mitchell, Dafnis Prieto and Oscar Hernandez, has its foundation in unraveling vertical constructs of culture: notions that have not only undermined sustainability for the individual artist, but also contributed an artifice in place of an authentic grasp of aesthetic development.

At the end of American Composers Forum's day-long Racial Equity and Inclusion Forum in Minnesota (American Composers Forum 2019),[4] President and CEO of the League of American Orchestras, Jesse Rosen, addressed the following proposition presented by an audience member: "There is a systematic problem of both unintended bias and blatant racism in orchestras who [sic] don't really want change, particularly audiences and boards ...." Rosen acquiesced, "Orchestras have a lot to answer for, there's no question about that. We have a history of active discrimination in our field, and we're living the legacy of that impact ... deep and extensive ... there's no mistake about that. And there are many people in orchestras who still like it to be pretty much the way it's been, and are not really advocating for change." Orchestras, according to a 2018 *New York Times* article, are among America's least racially diverse institutions (Cooper 2018). In a 2014 study, African American musicians made up only 1.8 percent of the nation's players. In a recent blog post, "Black Classical Composers Making News; Now Activate the Audiences," audience development expert Donna Walker Kuhne (2019) recounts a music critic's observation on the Philadelphia Orchestra's performance of flutist and composer Valerie Coleman's *Umoja, Anthem for Unity*. "That it took it 120 years of actively commissioning composers before landing on this demographic says a lot about how little the orchestra has noticed the city it has lived in all this time." It was the first time the orchestra had ever performed a classical work by a living African-American female composer.

Rosen's concluding remarks at the Equity Forum, in contrast, did not offer a promise of change nor an intervention for an inclusive future of the orchestral world; rather, he proceeded to defend the exclusionary nature of symphonic music: "Why do orchestras want to play dead white music? One of the reasons is that people want to hear it. It's the transactional reality ... I don't know how you tell kids in the three hundred youth orchestra in Venezuela that they are pillars of white supremacy, or the five professional orchestras in Mexico City that they are pillars of white supremacy ... in Soweto where

---

4   The complete live stream of the "2019 Racial Equity and Inclusion Forum" is available at https:// livestream.com/accounts/12638076/Artists4Equity/videos/195975002.

Mandela organized the African National Congress, where 60 of his colleagues were all shot to death ... the Minnesota Orchestra plays there." That the leader of the League was oblivious to the colonial legacy of symphonic orchestras, proselytizing forces of cultural imperialism in these former colonies, provoked a social media furor, exposing the music community's fragile tolerance for the League's failure at diversifying the field despite being allocated a disproportionate amount of arts funding. Additionally, Rosen missed the forty-five year ascendancy of El Sistema, a more authentic, hybrid and transformative adoption of Western Classical music in Venezuela. Through direct calls for Rosen's resignation, the League's position in the American cultural imagination for a moment became destabilized.

The fact that Rosen's tenure has lasted twenty-two years at the League was provided as further evidence that his leadership alone should be held responsible for the bureaucratic inertia. One Twitter post in particular seemed to align itself with Rosen's position. Dutch musicologist and artistic director of the NTR ZaterdagMatinee, Netherlands Public Broadcasting Company's concert series, the Netherlands Radio Philharmonic Orchestra, and the Netherlands Radio Choir, Kees Vlaardingerbroek (2019a), tweeted,

> In the 30s Nazi musicologist Heinrich Besseler fought against the Great
> Evil: 'The Jew'. Nowadays some American musicologists likewise want
> to purge the world of music. Their Great Enemy: 'The White Male'. So
> their approach is not just racist, but sexist as well. Progress indeed.

Vlaardingerbroek was as oblivious to Rosen's Jewish American identity as was Rosen, in his misappropriated proximity to the South African apartheid, in defending western symphonic orchestras in Soweto. Vlaardingerbroek (2019b) is also the author of "Bach was geen vrouw en westers. Nou en? Identiteitspolitiek rukt op in de muziekwereld" (Bach was not a woman and [is] western. So what? Identity policy is advancing in the music world). In this *deVolkskrant* article, Vlaardingerbroek warns the reader of the threat of identity politics imported from the US, and that "The dangers of this assault on heritage should not be underestimated .... A forced replacement of the great masters by female contemporaries or composers with non-European roots will irrevocably lead to destruction of public interest, to empty concert halls and eventually even their closure," a direct contrast to Walker Kuhne's optimism in the opportunity to revitalize an aging orchestra audience demographic by programming prominent Black composers. "Coleman's identity is an important factor to many, but especially to children all over who may never have this world was open to them—as composers and as listeners .... cultural organizations with the foresight to perform these works are being handed a wonderful opportunity to extend a welcoming invitation to communities of color ...." Whether the reverberations of equity, diversity, inclusion, and accessibility (EDIA) efforts are reviving old tropes of reverse racism in Holland or Minnesota, where a 1863 law still makes it illegal for the native Dakota people to live in the state, the US "melting pot" paradox is its greatest advantage in progressing the conversation toward a more equitable cultural ecology, while also actively unraveling the effects of structural racism in artistic production and reception.

Our willingness as cultural institutions to valiantly engage with our racial past can often be motivated through a cynical pitch for philanthropic dollars. In 2017, New York City (NYC), as culturally rich and diverse as it is segregated in public access to the arts, mandated data collection on the diversity of cultural institution staff, requiring arts organizations to submit meaningful goals in making their ranks more diverse. This initiative was motivated by evidence that most robust and thriving institutions were helmed by white male leaders. With a subway grid connecting virtually every NYC borough to the island of Manhattan, these mainstream institutions have come under criticism and scrutiny for their failure to engage audiences of color, and for their lack of sensitivity in creating an inclusive environment for these communities.

Recently, Carnegie Hall was one of the first to make a grand gesture celebrating NYC's immigrant legacy through an ambitious, citywide project, *Migrations: The Making of America*. Closer examination, however, reveals a sophisticated marketing sleight of hand. Over 137 events across NYC and its boroughs were programmed to engage audiences of color whom the institution has not had success cultivating. Only nine were actual main stage events at Carnegie Hall. Only four of those nine artists that the organization risked its curatorial and production resources toward were artists of color. Kevin Gover (Pawnee), director of the Museum of the American Indian at the Smithsonian, was featured in a promotional video, but Martha Redbone (Cherokee/Shawnee/Choctaw), the festival's only native artist, was relegated to an ancillary educational event. Community-based arts leaders who nurture diverse audiences in their venues despite the paucity or absence of funding support were forced to choose from a roster of artists contracted by Carnegie Hall, rather than being invited to participate in an advisory capacity for programming expertise within their own communities. The large institution's paternalistic approach exposed a superficial commitment to diversity. Instead of creating a welcoming gateway for audiences of color to fill the seats of their storied venues, Carnegie Hall, in pursuit of diversifying its branding, maintains its tradition of segregating and marginalizing audiences of color.

Since its *Statement of Commitment*, CMA now reports approximately 75 percent of its grant recipients are artists of color. Its presenting support effectively reaches organizations helmed by administrators of color, enabling them to continue fostering their authentic commitment to inclusivity within their audience communities. CMA was also featured in *Stanford Social Innovation Review* for "addressing inequities at the community level in creative, systemic ways." Diversifying applicant pools has resulted in diversifying the notion of *excellence*, and removing barriers in accessibility to CMA's grants applications is where we invest most of our resources and strategic thinking. The result has been many historic firsts for the organization, including the island of Puerto Rico receiving support to foster audience communities and artists for the first time in CMA's program history.

Blind spots haunt even the most effective strategic EDIA approaches. At a recent *Grantmakers in the Arts* conference in Denver, CO, non-profit leaders and members of the

Tlingit and Sicangu Lakota Native American tribes confronted a roomful of arts funders with a request: "if you are reaching zero native artists with your programs, and zero artists are applying, and consequently zero artists receive those grants, report it as such to your organizations, boards of directors and funders. This way we at least show up as a category." The specter of genocide and erasure of entire communities and historical practices creeps into our work as cultural advocates and arts administrators. The poet laureate Fred Moten casts Black existentialism on an Odysseus-like figure choosing a metaphoric state of homelessness over the "exigencies and brutalities that go with claiming the United States as presently construed and constructed as home .... Should we set out again, for some different place, for another world for another country, as [James] Baldwin would say, that we still have to make" (Columbia University Center for Teaching and Learning 2015).

As an advocate for an awe-inspiring community of jazz artists, I am allowed the privilege to participate in an ecology where artistic practice itself represents a microcosm of resistance. As administrators we can be a truly inclusive force with the realization that art reveals its true virtue as it thrives in its relational context. Yielding a quantifiable success rate in EDIA frameworks is best rooted in the philosophical thrust of our program design rather than the transactional value of adopting equity-based practices. We represent systems of absencing. The courage to disrupt our notions of *what* is credible in creative practice or *who* upholds artistic excellence, along with the vigilance toward ourselves and frequent re-evaluation of our programs has the possibility to inspire methodologies that nurture the individual artist and entirely transform creative habitats.

WORKS CITED

American Composers Forum. 2019. "2019 Racial Equity and Inclusion Forum." September 7. livestream.com/accounts/12638076/Artists4Equity/videos/195975002.

Bhabha, Homi.K. *The Location of Culture* New York, NY, Routledge, 1994.

Chamber Music America. 2017. "Statement of Commitment." January. https://www.chamber-music.org/statement-commitment.

Columbia University Center for Teaching and Learning. 2015. "Romare Bearden: A Black Odyssey | Fred Moten, University of California, Riverside, December 2, 2014." YouTube Video, 11:24. October 26. youtu.be/kiDudR513sw.

Cooper, Michael. 2018. "Seeking Orchestras in Tune With Their Diverse Communities." *New York Times*. April 18. www.nytimes.com/2018/04/18/arts/music/symphony-orchestra-diversity.html.

McCarthy, Kerry, and Maurine Knighton. 2019. "The Role of Philanthropy in Advancing Equity in the Arts." *Stanford Social Innovation Review*. October 7. www.ssir.org/articles/entry/the_role_of_philanthropy_in_advancing_equity_in_the_arts.

Vlaardingerbroek, Kees. 2019a. Twitter post, September 8, 2019, 5:54 a.m., twitter.com/KeesVlaar/status/11706515986929999168.

Vlaardingerbroek, Kees. 2019b. "Bach was geen vrouw en westers. Nou en? Identiteitspolitiek rukt op in de muziekwereld." *The Old Continent*. April 25, 2019. www.theoldcontinent.eu/kees-vlaardingerbroek-identity-politics-in-classical-music/.

Walker-Kuhne, Donna. 2019. "Black Classical Composers Making News; Now Activate the Audiences. International Communications Group, Inc." *Walker Communication Group* (blog). Accessed October 1. www.walkercommunicationsgroup.com/2019/10/20/black-classical-composers-making-news-now-activate-the-audiences/.

I'LL DO IT WHEN DAME JUDI DENCH DOES IT. SONG OF ROMANIA AND ARTS COUNCIL ENGLAND: A QUESTION OF PUBLIC ENGAGEMENT, RELEVANCE, AND DIVERSITY IN THEATRE MAKING

MIHAI FLOREA
University of Bristol

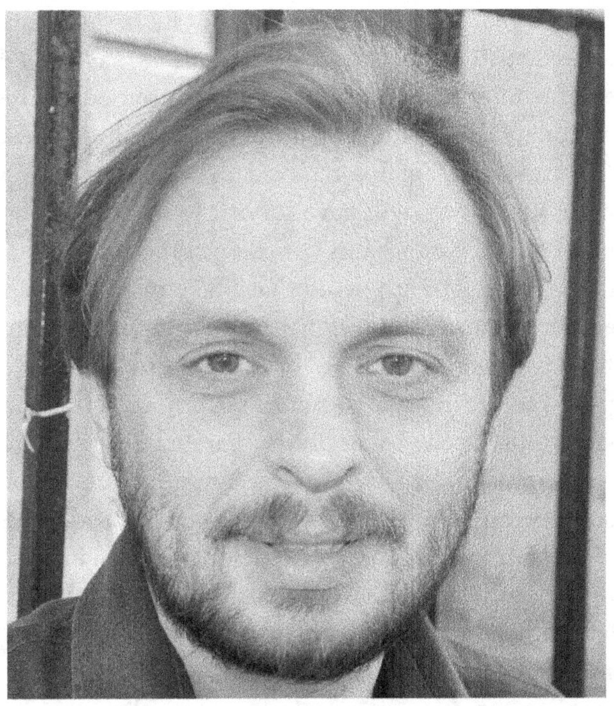

Mihai Florea is professional actor and a part-time teacher/researcher in Theatre Studies at University of Bristol, UK, and recipient of a Duignan bursary for a PhD thesis titled Actor in a Second Language. He has presented academic papers at a number of universities in the UK, Finland, Germany and Lithuania. He is an Associate Member of the Brokering Intercultural Exchange group, a global network of academics and cultural managers, and a co-founder of Nu Nu, a theatre company that supports professional actors who use English as a second (non-native) language. He also established and coordinates CASL (Centre for Actors in a Second Language), an online research tool dedicated to the theme of second language acting. One of his articles, entitled 'Egg-fying' Hamlet: The Second Language Actor and Shakespeare Grammaticality" has appeared in April 2019, in Shakespeare Jahrbuch 155. The article entitled 'BANDIT: Here to Haunt You! On Why I Became an Émigré Theatre Maker'—was published in 2019 in Journal MIK

—Art History and Criticism Reviews, published by the Faculty of Arts, Vytautas Magnus University, Kaunas, Lithuania. The piece 'Collaborating with a stick: Algernon Schtick Meets Nina Bambina' will be published in 2020 in 'The Oxford Artistic & Practice Based Research Platform.' An article titled: 'Un-bonsai-ing my bonsai: a plant-based adaptation of Oresteia' is currently in preparation.

ABSTRACT

The purpose of this article is to thoroughly interrogate the source of Nu Nu theatre artists' anxiety and suspiciousness vis-à-vis ACE's public engagement, relevance, and diversity requirements. The aim is to determine if our anxiety is totally unfounded or if, on the contrary, it is a response to less detectable nuances in ACE's funding philosophy. Inevitably, the discussion will have to visit graver questions, like what makes (or is) an artist? or what is (or can be) the role of an artist in society? In this context, the approach that I take might appear somewhat unexpected. I link the sentiment of anxiety vis-à-vis funding from ACE to the cultural propaganda that we, Nu Nu's artists, were (often subliminally) exposed to during our communist and post-communist lives in Romania. More precisely, I will draw a parallel between ACE's public engagement, relevance, and diversity requirements, and the ideology of the large-scale cultural and artistic event organised under the control of the Romanian Communist Party, called Song of Romania. The working hypothesis is that the anxiety and suspiciousness felt versus ACE's demands might indicate nothing more than an unresolved post-traumatic, post-communist fearfulness. Therefore, there is a danger that this article might be just a paranoid reaction triggered by a distant, traumatic, and unresolved past. Nonetheless, that might not be the case.

Keywords: Theatre, public engagement, diversity

LO HARÉ CUANDO LA DAMA JUDI DENCH LO HAGA. SONG OF ROMANIA Y ARTS COUNCIL ENGLAND: UNA CUESTIÓN DE COMPROMISO PÚBLICO, RELEVANCIA Y DIVERSIDAD EN LA CREACIÓN DE TEATRO

RESUMEN

El propósito de este artículo es interrogar a fondo la fuente de ansiedad y sospecha de los artistas de teatro de Nu Nu en relación con los requisitos de participación pública, relevancia y diversidad de ACE. El objetivo es determinar si nuestra ansiedad es totalmente infundada o si, por el contrario, es una respuesta a matices menos detectables en la filosofía de financiación de ACE. Inevitablemente, la discusión tendrá que visitar preguntas más graves, como ¿qué hace (o es) un artista? o cuál es (o puede ser) el papel de un artista en la sociedad? En este contexto, el enfoque que adopto puede parecer algo inesperado. Relaciono el sentimiento de ansiedad con respecto a la financiación de ACE con la propaganda cultural a la que nosotros, los artistas de Nu Nu, estuvimos (a menudo subliminalmente) expuestos durante nuestras vidas comunistas y poscomunistas en Rumania. Más precisamente, trazaré un paralelismo entre los requisitos de participación pública, relevancia y diversidad de ACE, y la ideología del evento cultural y artístico a gran escala organizado bajo el control del Partido Comunista Rumano, llamado Song of Romania. La hipótesis de trabajo es que la ansiedad y la desconfianza que se sienten frente a las demandas de ACE podrían indicar nada más que un miedo postraumático y poscomunista no resuelto. Por lo tanto, existe el peligro de que este artículo sea solo una reacción paranoica desencadenada por un pasado distante, traumático y sin resolver. Sin embargo, ese podría no ser el caso.

Palabras clave: Teatro, compromiso público, diversidad

我追随女爵士朱迪·丹奇。"罗马尼亚之歌"与英国艺术委员会：关于戏剧制作中公共参与、相关性和多样性的疑问

摘要

本文旨在全面调查与英国艺术委员会（ACE）的公共参与、相关性及多样性要求相关的Nu Nu戏剧艺术家的焦虑和多疑来源。目的是确定我们（即Nu Nu艺术家）的焦虑是否全然毫无根据，或者相反，焦虑是对ACE资助理念中较少被探测的细微变化的一种响应。不可避免地，探讨部分将审视更严峻的疑问，例如造就一名艺术家的是什么（或者艺术家是什么）？或者艺术家在社会中的作用（能）是什么？以此为背景，我采用的方法可能看似有些出乎意料。我将关于ACE资助的焦虑情绪与我们在罗马尼亚共产主义及后共产主义生活期间所接触的文化宣传相联系（这种接触通常是潜意识的）。更确切地，我将把ACE的公共参与、相关性及多样性要求，与由罗马尼亚共产党控制下组织的大范围文化艺术事件的意识形态（称之为"罗马尼亚之歌"）进行类比。假设认为，相对于ACE的资助要求，焦虑与多疑可能仅表明一种尚

未解决的、创伤后的、具有后共产主义性质的恐惧。因此，一个坏的可能性则是，本文可能是对一个遥远的、痛苦的、有待克服的过去的一种偏执反应。但也有可能不是这样。

关键词：戏剧，公共参与，多样性

1. INTRODUCTION

Nu Nu Theatre was established in Bristol, UK in 2012 by two Romanian professional theatre-makers. Ileana Gherghina and I were both born in communist Romania and spent most of our youth in the much-detested and much-contested period of transition from a communist to a capitalist society. In 2008, we two theatre-makers decided to move to the UK for good. Here, we begun to timidly produce theatre work and as such, have several times applied (under Nu Nu Theatre's banner) for funds from the Arts Council England (ACE). Such funds were expected to cover production costs, artists' wages for specific periods of time, and unexpected production-related spending. ACE expects all projects submitted for funding to fulfil specific criteria. Most importantly, the applicant needs to convince the funder that the proposed work engages with, is relevant to, and includes at some point during development, creation, and presentation as many and as diverse members of the wider public as possible. Particular attention is given to participants coming from disadvantaged backgrounds and to people with very little prior engagement in/with the arts. In the words of an ACE representative, what is expected is that the funded project will engage its participants in life-changing experiences: "For example, a workshop has the potential to be life-changing for its six workshop participants" (Kapadia 2019). ACE's candid ambition for life-changing experiences (in exchange for funding) in the short space of a few workshops (how many workshops can an artist conduct when, for instance, the funding for an entire small-scale theatre production is around £10,000, including artist fees?) is somewhat bewildering through its apparent mercantilism. On the other hand, the expectation that the funded artist will shake the participants' conscience (even though they may not have had any prior contact with that art form) brings to mind Eugene Ionesco's bitter exchange with the reputed theatre critic Kenneth Tynan:

> I beseech you, Mr Tynan, to not attempt—with art or other means—to improve the fate of man. I am begging you! We've had enough civil wars up to now, and blood, and tears, and unfair trials, and "just" executioners, and "vile" martyrs, and dashed hopes and prisons. Do not seek to improve man's fate, if you really wish him well. (Ionesco 1992:126)

It is by now probably evident that the funder's expectations vis-à-vis public engagement/relevance and diversity have awoken in us, the artists of Nu Nu Theatre, feelings of suspicion and anxiety. There is—I argue—an unhealthy dose of prescriptivism behind the good intentions of the funder: detectable both in the mercantilist approach and in the misconstrued view that artists can somehow deliver mind-blowing experiences with the snap of the fingers. The particular expectations of the funder have haunted the way we have dreamed about, structured, and written about (on the application form) our future projects. The submission of an application for funding from ACE has influenced the way that we felt obliged to re-evaluate and question—in light of the funder's expectations —the dream/idea behind our proposed project. This tedious process of re-editing and re-writing our ideas in order to get money often results in a sense of having lost sense of what had initially "moved" us to do that particular project. The overall sentiment is that the application process perfidiously takes charge of our imagination, displacing us as makers of the project. As such, we often prefer not to apply for ACE funding at all and resort to various other survival stratagems.

The purpose of this article is to thoroughly interrogate the source of our anxiety and suspiciousness vis-à-vis ACE's public engagement, relevance, and diversity requirements. The aim is to determine if our anxiety is totally unfounded or if, on the contrary, it is a response to less detectable nuances in ACE's funding philosophy. Inevitably, the discussion will have to visit graver questions, like what makes (or is) an artist? or what is (or can be) the role of an artist in society? In this context, the approach that I take might appear somewhat unexpected. I link the sentiment of anxiety vis-à-vis funding from ACE to the cultural propaganda that we, Nu Nu's artists, were (often subliminally) exposed to during our communist and post-communist lives in Romania. Concomitantly, the working hypothesis is that the anxiety and suspiciousness felt versus ACE's demands might indicate nothing more than an unresolved post-traumatic, post-communist fearfulness. Therefore, there is a danger that this article might be just a paranoid reaction triggered by a distant, traumatic, and unresolved past.

To begin with, it must be noted that all artistic and cultural activities in communist Romania were subject to state supervision, censure, and control by representatives of the Party. Consequently, all such activities were exposed to contamination from Party political dogma. In conditions of relentless surveillance, Romanian intellectuals and artists festered an acute suspiciousness towards any kind of institutional language or guidance/ advice/order coming from above. Like a high-resolution scanning device, they directed a ray of cynical hypersensitivity towards anything emanating from the Communist Party and its numerous representatives: intellectuals and artists were on alert for inherently manipulative prescriptions emanating from the elusive above. Eugene Ionesco—in *Present Past Past Present*—aptly describes this kind of situation:

> You can create a fleas' circus. They will need to be trained, and the initial aim is that the fleas stop jumping. How to do that? The fleas are placed under a glass. They will try to jump, hit the glass wall, fall back. But from one point onwards, the fleas will stop jumping. The glass can now be lifted. And behold, the fleas are now advancing dizzily, alienated; they

> can now be pushed, blown over but they won't jump anymore. (Ionesco
> 1993:160)

I dare say that Ionesco was wrong only in one way: whilst he perfectly describes the conditions and methods imposed/utilised by a(ny) totalitarian regime (seeking a political dressage of its citizens), he errs when describing the fleas as being reduced to catatonic, disabled, and dizzied entities. What Ionesco did not intuit was that many of the fleas trapped in the circus had metamorphosed into cynical beings, triggering their ultimate survival mechanism. With laser-sharp attention fixed on the dressage "master," the fleas return to the catacombs of cynicism and suspicion in order to resist, expecting a very distant liberation. Such irony-laden, suspicious moods have continued to characterise intellectuals, artists, and normal citizens in Romania long after the fall of communism. Romanian citizens to this day display great mistrust towards political institutions (Parliament, national government, local government, and their representatives).

This deeply embedded cynicism has probably rubbed off on us too—the émigré artists of Nu Nu—and it has now become manifest in our attitude vis-à-vis ACE's expectations from a funded artist. Such a particular state of mind (this time seen in relation to the wider question of Eastern and Western Europe united by the EU) is aptly described by poet and former dissident Ana Blandiana, in a speech given at the Babeş-Bolyai University, in Cluj, in 2016:

> Those eyes that were trained for decades to sharpen their vision in darkness finally got accustomed to the light of freedom. It was observed though that those who had encountered the totalitarian dogma could not be convinced as easily as Western intellectuals to accept another type of dogmatism, no matter how noble its intentions were. At the end of the day, Communism was too the tragic materialisation of a beautiful utopia. (Blandiana 2016)

Therefore, this article is underpinned by a fear of manipulation inherited from a distant past: it consists of a keen, paranoid search for details that might identify state/political dogma or any intent to instrumentalise the artist's expressive freedom, by seeking to subsume it to political and other kinds of agendas.

One additional question that characterises this article is: can the funded artist—faced with all the additional filters imposed by the funder (deadlines, diversity requirements, the extra chores of engaging with certain members of the community, etc.)—ever retain and act upon his/her artistic freedom? Evidently, the underlying preoccupation refers to the relevance and indeed the value of artistic freedom—the freedom to do whatever the fuck I dream about without you, the funder, holding me accountable in any way or demanding something in return for your money. Throughout the article, I define artistic freedom in a gradual fashion, adding extra nuances as the argument progresses. I start by quoting Felix Guattari's concept of the "value of creation":

Today, a technological innovation or a scientific equation will take its value from the register of exchange values if it can be found useful in the immediate process of production. But there are also values of aesthetic and scientific creation that do not have an immediate effect on exchange values and which, for this reason, actually deserve being funded. (Guattari 2015:31)

Artistic freedom is therefore an innovative mode of investigating life/existence, whose trajectory and effects cannot be fully quantifiable (or covered) in terms of political, social, or economic impact. At the same time, the value that artistic freedom produces cannot be immediately convertible through a measure of its potential usefulness to the wider society or to particular individuals. As such, it seems fair to imagine that one great concern for both the artist and the funder (for different reasons, evidently) is whether artistic freedom is a fundable thing.

In order to bring all these important questions under the purview of the paranoid critical eye, I attempt a comparative exercise between a famous cultural/artistic manifestation of the communist era, called *Song of Romania* (*Cântarea României*), and ACE's public engagement, relevance, and diversity strategy. With regards to ACE, I am particularly interested in how the themes of public engagement, relevance, and diversity are outlined and "languaged" (Jacobsen 2018:18) in the application form and/or explanatory materials.

2. SONG OF ROMANIA: AESTHETIC RATATOUILLE

Song of Romania (*Cântarea României*) appeared as a result of the *XI Congress of the Romanian Communist Party* (*Congresul al XI-lea al Partidului Comunist Român*), organised in 1974, and launched the idea of "the creation of a multilaterally-developed socialist society and Romania's advancement towards Communism" (Congress XI 1975:614). *Song of Romania* was imagined as a cultural and artistic event of great magnitude, delivered in the form of a large-scale (countrywide) festival, structured as a series of competitions run at local, regional, and national levels and comprising artistic manifestations of all genres. *Song of Romania* was a biannual event that lasted from 1976 to 1989, with seven editions in total. To give a sense of the size of the festival, it is sufficient to note that it grew exponentially from two million participants during its first edition to around five million participants in 1989.

The huge numbers fulfilled Nicolae Ceausescu's vision:

The emergence of the new man presupposes the collaboration of activists, [...] with the large masses of those who work, and on that basis, the creation of an ample popular movement in the domains of education and culture. Like in all sectors of material and spiritual life, the determinant role in the creation of the new culture belongs to the popular masses, to the unending, always innovative popular genius. (Ceausescu 1976:52)

The underlying aim of the Communist Party was to allow the masses into the process of artistic creation, which in turn would (supposedly) ensure an intensification and diversification of the cultural life of the country. *Song of Romania* would thus validate the Party's strange theory: they believed in a national culture emerging from the masses and pitted against the bourgeois, "anti-revolutionary" artistic/intellectual elites. Arts and culture would now finally and fully "contribute to the education of the entire society, of the youth, in the spirit of endless labor for the growth of socialism in Romania" (Scînteia 1976:1). The Romanian Communist Party wanted to realise in practice the rather peculiar idea (which later on metamorphosed into an outright obsession) that working people cannot simply be neutral, silent beneficiaries and spectators of artistic acts or cultural activities. Quite the opposite, they need to take on the role of co-creators (if not sole originators) of the artistic/cultural act. The onus was put on them creating the much-praised communist "new man": no longer ignoble, simple workers, but rather revolutionary creators of civilisation, art, and culture and architects of a long-awaited glorious era of equality, prosperity, and peace. *Song of Romania* unified—in a single platform—the regime's keen interest to promote a new type of art and culture, with the phantasmagorical prototype of a "new, multilaterally-developed man" (the actual expression used by Communist Party authorities). The new man could by no means remain just a maker/producer of agricultural or industrial goods, but would become the artisan of a totally new artistic and cultural dawn. For that to happen, art (with its "bourgeois" elites of professionals) needed to be subsumed under the political discourse of progress.

The thinking behind *Song of Romania* encouraged most of all a quantitative expansion of the (so-called) cultural/artistic activity throughout the country, the focus being to involve ever-more working people in the act of artistic creation: people in the factories, in the fields, and on the farms were targeted. *Song of Romania* was preaching a type of art "inspired by the contemporary realities, by the history of our people, by the glorious past of our Party and of the working class" (Scînteia 1976:1). This could be achieved through an exponential, grandiloquent, and large-scale increase of popular participation in artistic performances and cultural manifestations. The masses—be they workers in factories or in the fields—had an obligation, as part of their job descriptions, to prepare various artistic "moments" for presentation in the *Song of Romania* festival. To that effect, everybody was (warmly or less so) encouraged to join the factory's or village's folk-dance group, amateur theatre group, etc. All participant industries, state institutions, factories, etc. would thus become involved in "promot[ing] a revolutionary and efficiently educative art" (Scînteia 1976:1). From the onset, the great festival was programmed to be eminently inclusive: the manifestation would reverberate—on its very wide performative canvas—in the much-claimed social unity of the entire Romanian people (who rallied behind the Party, of course). Diversity would be reaffirmed through celebratory kitsch and the false unity displayed during the gargantuan event: anybody and everybody regardless of ethnicity or social origin were included, except of course the "bourgeois" artistic elites.

Throughout the entire communist era and particularly at the time when *Song of Romania* was in existence, intellectuals and professional artists in particular were pressed by one grave concern. They feared that the festival—through its force-fed diversity and absurdly wide-reaching levels of participation and engagement—was mixing professional artists with amateurs and non-artists entering the stage straight from factories, shop floors, or the fields. In its politically motivated obsession with portraying the working man as *the* authentic creator of art, the state turned its full attention to amateur artists and non-artists to the detriment of professional artists. The professional's role remained only that of safeguarding, nurturing, and supporting the yet-undiscovered genius of the working man: "Professional artistic institutions grant qualified support to amateur artists collaborating with them in order to increase the qualitative level of the performance" (Scînteia 1976:1).

The festival therefore functioned as an efficient instrument for depriving professional artists of their traditional status of innovators and creators of artistic work. Their aspirations, dreams, and creativity were deliberately diluted in the cacophonic soup of amateurisms and non-professional, semi-artistic, and proto-folkloric activities of *Song of Romania*. The professional artist's message, expressed in a clearly articulated, skilful artistic discourse, was thus trivialised and lost. Professional artists saw *Song of Romania* as the regime's perfidious way to deprive them of their basic identity, that of experts in a particular field of art. The Communist Party's paternalistic, derogatory attitude towards professional artists is encapsulated in the words of painter Sabin Bălaşa (himself an uneasy supporter of the regime's thinking on art): "The artist's personal happiness cannot be conceived but in the context of the happiness of the country's entire community" (Bălaşa 1975:4). How can that ever be true, when artistic freedom is not a question of happiness, but instead of investigating existence in all its peaks and pitfalls?

Professional artists suffered due to *Song of Romania*, lost as they were in a sea of pseudo-artistic activities. From an aesthetic point of view, the festival was indubitably kitsch on the grandest of scales. On the same stage there would appear, in succession, ballerinas, folk instrument players, military school students, artistic brigades from factories, folk dancers, mountain rangers, and Party activists, followed by choirs and poetry recitals. The festival was an aesthetic ratatouille. The audiences' artistic taste was as such profoundly affected, given the illogical amalgam of genres, competencies, and talent on display. The expression *Song of Romania* was eventually adopted into arts circles' parlance and used to denote the dubious artistic value of a particular artwork, show, film, etc. "This is like *Song of Romania!*" a vexed theatre critic would exclaim, condemning the aesthetic mishmash of a certain theatre performance. *Song of Romania* sought to put in practice what I argue to be the unfounded and dangerous idea that anyone can become an artist when and if the Party says so. At the time, subversively or less so, this way of thinking had been sanctioned by intellectuals and artists alike as dangerously utopian and as a political instrumentalisation of art.

3. ARTS COUNCIL ENGLAND: PUBLIC ENGAGEMENT, RELEVANCE, AND DIVERSITY

In this world and era, public engagement, relevance, and diversity are prerequisites to any successful application to ACE and its funding streams. The concept of diversity in the arts became popular during New Labour, after Tony Blair's election in 1997. It was anticipated by the Macpherson report, which made seventy recommendations for eradicating institutional racism within the police. In the arts, the movement for diversity inspired the creation of bodies such as the UK film Council (2000) or Cultural Diversity Network (2000) that were intended to uphold diversity within television. As Clive Nwonka (2019) notes in *The Guardian*, "The vision was of arts and culture having a therapeutic effect on marginalized communities."

The theme of public engagement and relevance is intertwined with the vision for diversity, as detailed in the *Creative Case for Diversity*, launched in 2011. ACE is focused on "engaging the arts and culture sector nationwide to reinforce the importance of diversity in art, arts leadership and audiences" (Unlimited 2016). Funded artists must therefore pay increased attention to ACE's programme of radical inclusiveness and diversity so that their work reflects the incredible diversity of contemporary British society. That means that every cultural/artistic event funded by ACE should demonstrate its response to the diversities, histories, opportunities, and provocations of the specific local communities in which the funded project is produced and/or performed. Similarly, any cultural/artistic activity funded should be faithful to the principle of including minorities and socially marginalised people as participants and ideally as co-creators of the artistic project. ACE motivates its requirements for public engagement and diversity with the fact that the organisation is put in charge of public money. The British state (through successive governments) has assumed a discourse of greater inclusivity, diversity, and relevance of the arts and by way of consequence, all funded projects must submit to the aforementioned principles, as ACE's Cate Canniffe eloquently explained:

> ACE is a subcontractor for the government, so they simply need to respect certain procedures and require certain information to report it to the government. [...] ACE has the duty to hold to account on diversity and inclusion, so they intervene to make sure this has been abided by. (Shishkova 2019:2)

Whilst the aims of diversity and public engagement are laudable, the language that articulates them may appear (to a paranoid interpreter such as myself) particularly utopian. The problem is that ACE's targets of diversity and inclusivity belong to the realm of the theoretical discourse and not to the realm of praxis: these aims seem conceived not by artists/practitioners but by managers and administrators of money and language. In a certain sense, the language employed by the Romanian Communist Party with regards to arts does not differ very much—in its power to articulate politically motivated discourse—from that of ACE: a similar prescriptivism, a similar imposition of utopian outcomes upon the work of the artist, and a similar sense that the funder seeks to control and direct the artist's work. There is a similarly militant tone employed vis-à-vis marginalised members of the community (communists were obsessed with workers); there is the inclination to pre-empt, to generously indicate directions, to formulate expected outcomes, and to preach to the artist about the role of art in society. ACE's policies seem to originate from above (from the makers of theories about art) rather than from below (from the artists, from those who actually make art). For example, Lyn Gardner (writer and critic for *The Guardian*) speaks at length about the role that theatres should embrace in the new century. Tormented by this existential matter (akin to Kenneth Tynan, whom Ionesco implored to stop trying to right society's ills through art) and exhilarated by the solutions she manages to find, Gardner enlists directives (ambitious and well-intentioned, just like those of the Romanian Communist Party). In her view, theatres will have "re-think and re-imagine their purpose in the twenty-first century" and consider "who they serve, but also around who they do not yet serve and how they can address that" (Gardner 2019:2-3). Why should art (theatre in this case) be put into the service of an ideal, no matter how noble that ideal might be? Why should theatre be programmed to serve a particular social purpose? Gardner warns that "the danger is that unless theatre embraces a wider civic role, it will simply come to be seen as increasingly out of touch and elitist" (Gardner 2019:3). But what if, on the contrary, theatre needs to become even more distanced from the reach of the masses in order to preserve its uniqueness with respect to other media and other arts in this unpredictable century? Why shouldn't theatre be out of touch (perhaps even as a form of conservation and self-reinvention) and be allowed to control its own value of creation? Why should theatre move in tune with fashion? Gardner is concerned with what she calls the "civic role" of theatre:

> How can theatres and other arts organisations fulfil a civic role, engage
> with their communities, and find different ways to be fully embedded
> in their locale? How can they start behaving less like monasteries and
> more like town squares, a place to which everyone has access, and every-
> one is welcome? (Gardner 2019:3)

But where is it written that theatre should be a place for everyone? Are the studies in high mathematics less relevant or less useful to wider society simply because they are accessible only to an elite of monk-like mathematicians? Should philosophical discussions be broadcast in the marketplace, as otherwise they might risk being seen as not fulfilling a civic role? Should everything be for everybody? Should everything be measured for its worth in terms of civic role? Where does the assumption that art belongs to or should be accessed by everybody come from?

Furthermore, the *Creative Case for Diversity* stresses the idea that diversity is a key factor in the "dynamic that drives art forward, that innovates it and brings it closer to and in a more authentic dialogue with contemporary society" (Mahamdallie 2012). ACE's proposition is, I argue, problematic, since artistic activity, produced under the impulse of what I call artistic freedom, is always directly linked to the unpredictable investigations of the artist. These investigations (produced outside theoretical discourse about art) do not move forward or backward and most importantly, do not move as the funder would wish to: the investigative journeys simply exist, describing trajectories steeped in freedom. As Gilles Deleuze and Felix Guattari note, artistic creation points to "the constitution of an earth and a people that are lacking" (Deleuze et al. 1994:108). Art occupies itself with creating "a possibility of life" (Deleuze 1997:4) and should not therefore be primarily concerned with its civic, social, or political role. In other words, artistic acts contain possibilities of life, which go beyond the socioeconomic and political arrangements of the day. Perhaps that is why many totalitarian regimes (and other types) fear the arts and artists, as they are able to propose new possibilities of life, outside, different from, and better than the status quo. The secret ingredient to provoking such new possibilities is artistic freedom.

At this point, it is useful to further explicate the way I envisage artistic freedom. Artistic freedom is the sole generator of value of creation, which, as we have seen, stands outside the register of exchange values coordinated by the state (through ACE). In other words, artistic freedom is unrecognisable in the funder's (or the state's) utilitarian register of expectations (the expectation that theatre should be like a town square, for example). Artistic freedom can be explained like such: I make theatre because I want to, not because I am on a mission to save my neighbour or because I want to improve the social conditions around me. I sing because I sing. Art represents a qualitative jump outside life as we know it. It is a branching out into an alternative equation of existence, adding elements (types of people or kinds of life) that are currently lacking. It is precisely artistic freedom that the state and its funding intermediaries want to capture and use for their register of exchange values, putting it to work for their various agendas.

Bearing that in mind, how can ACE talk about art as moving forward? Has art ever remained behind the times? How can that be conceivable if, as seen, art deals only with possibilities of life? Has art ever gone backwards, when we know for sure that even in the darkest times, artists have pointed towards previously unhoped for, undreamed of worlds and types of people that are lacking? Art, therefore, cannot be seen as moving forward or backwards on a horizontal axis. Instead, it engenders new axes, puncturing the stratosphere of life as we know it, creating openings into worlds that until then had been lacking. These leaps into unexpected referential systems that offer new colour to our existence cannot be contained in a geometry of horizontal lines in which we measure either progress or regress (proportionally to how "civic" an artistic act is). Artistic freedom involves a lightning bolt, high-voltage electricity that punctures through the circumstances of the present. That leads us back to the question of art's so-called "authentic dialogue with contemporary society." Talking about art in these terms is completely erroneous—there can be no measure of authenticity fixed in art's dialogue with the wider society. If one day a theatre-maker or actor decides to walk the streets of Bristol reciting lines from Christopher Marlowe, does that put him/her in a less authentic dialogue with contemporary society than another artist who writes a play about the financial strains of people in a particular Bristol community? Every artistic act generates a new axis oriented towards the "cosmos (or the future)" (Young et al. 2013:169). In practice (as opposed to talking about artistic practice), the idea of an authentic dialogue with contemporary society is out of the question: all dialogue (as long as it creates possibilities of life) is contemporary, authentic, and relevant, even if it speaks about people who died during the plague or about the feelings of amoebas. There is no measure of contemporaneity, authenticity, or relevance when art punctures the known/familiar to disclose alternative universes: all these values are intrinsic to the artistic practice and do not need to be displayed at the request of an external force (the funder, in this case). Anything that might limit artistic freedom keeps art on a horizontal axis. Later, I deal with the question of how art leaps from contemporary socio-political realities to overcoming them and creating relevance, authenticity, and contemporaneity on a different plane.

Similarly, diversity is a value that is imposed at the level of discourse (rather than enabled practically, as I exemplify later) on the artistic process. Here is one example of the type of language/discourse of diversity and inclusion circulated by arts organisations and charities in the UK:

> A continuous drive for equality is imperative to remove barriers in the art world, releasing and realising potential and helping to transform the arts so that they truly reflect the reality of the diverse country that we have become but still do not fully recognise. (Unlimited 2016)

Doesn't such militant, energising, and triumphalist languaging resemble the mobilising messages of the Communist Party in Romania, in the seventies? Isn't this bureaucratic, slogan-saturated, wooden language (it was called wooden language in communist Romania) the coffin of imagination for any artist wanting to apply for funding? Or is it just my paranoid reading of an otherwise generous stance? Art possesses the inherent power (inscribed in the value of creation, energised by artistic freedom)—in its search for arranging chaos through "affects, percepts and blocs of sensations" (Young et al. 2013:169)—to do away with the barriers between people, races, and cultures by proposing a new way of life and types of people that are currently lacking. The moment that art is instructed from above about which types of possible (diverse) worlds are desirable, artistic freedom is arrested and lost. Similarly, art does not need to be transformed, as it engenders its own transformation and liberation: "Art consists of liberating the life that man has imprisoned. Man never ceases to imprison life, he does not cease to kill life. The artist is the one who liberates a life" (Deleuze 2007).

The confusion that the discourse of both *Song of Romania* and ACE propagates is the following: the barriers existent in art institutions have very little to do with art or with the artists themselves, but everything with to do with the complex bureaucracies, policies, policymaking, theorising, and languaging that oversee money, the management of institutions, and, most of all, the discourse about the role of art in society. All such, bureaucracies will always be tributary to various governments, councils, counsels, and so forth, and their agendas will never be primarily concerned with proposing an Earth and a type of people that are lacking. They will be eager to motivate their expenditures through assessments of impact and immediately measurable utility. That explains Ana Blandiana's poetic, yet valid, point: "Had it been created by the poets our world would have looked radically different" (Blandiana 2016). Diversity must be created at a practical level, from the bottom up, by the artists themselves, and not imposed through a detached, rhetorical discourse on diversity. Diversity is a diversity of worlds and people who are lacking, not diversity on a piece of paper.

The artist cannot be made tributary to such bureaucracies and policies: artists are tributary to affirming their experience of moving like a lightning bolt through chaos, towards the liberation of a possible life. In this way, artists serve the community in all its diversity, from below, because their quest is oriented towards the liberation of new understandings about the prisons in which we (with our own diverse bureaucracies) consistently lock ourselves.

There is also (deliberate?) confusion between equal access/participation to the arts/culture infrastructure and equal access to the artistic act. Judi Dench cannot be asked to create her roles alongside amateurs or non-artists in a community centre somewhere in rural England: it is the non-artists (or amateurs) who need to be allowed entrance to the National or to the Old Vic to see Dench rehearsing/playing her roles. Amateurs/non-artists must be given access to all the necessary instruments and funding if they want to become a professional. I return to the question of techne (vocation, knowledge, and expertise in the arts-making process) in the fourth part of this article. I only note here that encouraging participation in and co-creation of the artistic art (which leads to mixing various degrees of expertise and professional with non-professional abilities, like the *Song of Romania* model) can never enhance the quality of the artistic act. On the contrary, it drags it into the ground, into the banal, overturning its real aim, which is that of lightning bolting through chaos on ever-new axes. The mixing of competencies and abilities under the banner of diversity and engagement denies the emergence of a "deterritorialized plane from chaos to the cosmos" (Young et al. 2013:169), trivialising it. As the artistic act is pushed into quantitative growth (engaging more people and co-authors of various competencies), the process always loses its sharpness and focus.

With this kind of language regarding diversity/public engagement in and through the arts, we are clearly in the territory of the instrumentalisation of art, expected to serve the state's (neoliberal) theorisation of desired/imagined social and political outcomes. Art can of course help clarify or better frame matters that are often of a political or social nature, but it can never be asked to solve them. That is not art's role or its power. As Deleuze and Guattari note, the job of art is to "deterritorialize the system of opinion that brought together dominant perceptions and affections within a natural, historical, and social milieu" (Deleuze et al. 1994:197). Art cannot be rendered captive—under the civic duty banner—to the dominant perceptions and affections (existent, unbalanced socio-political and economic conditions identified by ACE). Art's role is to surpass discourses about art, by undergoing a qualitative jump (the search for the possible) onto always a different axis. Art could not transform Romania's working classes into communist new men and art will not be able to save the disadvantaged and marginalised in the capitalist UK society from their plight.

> Diversity must become not an optional extra but part of the fabric of our discussions and decisions. Let us banish forever the wrong notion that diversity in the arts is a problem. It is in fact a map to all our futures. (Unlimited 2016)

An artist's work must be overshadowed by the requirement for diversity or relevance. That amounts to a politically driven imposition upon the artistic act, which should not be confused with the political character of the artistic act. Hannah Arendt identifies theatre as "the political art par excellence" (*Arendt 1998:*188). The distinction that I make is the following: the terrain from which the artistic act shoots off is evidently determined by economic and socio-political markers. Secondly, the effects of the artistic act (its echoes) attain, through subsequent interpretation, a political nature. However, the act itself (the lightning bolt) exists outside and beyond the political. A coin has two sides, but it cannot be said that the coin *is* the two sides. The source/terrain of an artistic act and its subsequent reverberations are political, but the core of the act (the artistic act itself) is not political. Undoubtedly, any artistic act draws its inspiration, energy of revolt, and references from concrete political or social circumstances, but these pass through the filter of artistic freedom, which produces a disruptive, unprogrammable amalgamation and deterritorialisation, an unhinging and reorientation towards unexpected, random axes. The effect of this process returns as an echo to the reality on the ground, as it were, and creates subsequent political reverberations and interpretations. Fuelled by artistic freedom, the artistic act is political in the way it opposes the political (or social, etc.) references that it used as launching pad to the possible life and people that appear thereafter. It may also be noted that to explore new, possible worlds is an act of criticism of the current world, and therefore a political act. Like Arendt, this argument appears to say that theatre's core is political. I argue instead that at theatre's core lies not the political, but the random algorithms with which artistic freedom deterritorialises the political to transfigure it onto a different axis (the effects of the appearance of this new axis can be interpreted as political). If theatre had a political core, it would cease to be theatre and would instead be politics.

For the communists, it was important to demonstrate—using art—that their utopian social system was perfectly valid (thus justifying the violent way the political system had been imposed on Romania). For ACE (and ultimately the state for whom ACE acts as an intermediary), the idea of diversity is just part of a wider political discourse. As Clive Nwonka (2019) notes in his article *The Arts were Supposed to Champion Diversity. What Went Wrong?*, the diversity strategy "employs language to conceal the pathological inequality and exclusionary labour processes at the sector's heart." As such, Nwonka notes, all political meaning is extracted from the concept of diversity: it is neutralised by being turned into theoretical discourse. A purely social and political agenda for diversity would have to identify an issue with certain artists being systematically marginalised because of their race, ethnicity, social status, etc. This would render diversity a question of social justice as opposed to an issue of simply including marginalised artists into a particular creative sector, for specific projects. For instance, non-British actors (like Nu Nu's actors) are not invited to the National Theatre London to audition alongside their native counterparts for all the roles available. Non-native actors are employed only for specific theatre projects that seek to make a point about diversity.

The state (at least its neoliberal side) is not—it seems—primarily interested in making access to the arts infrastructure and funding more equal for all artists. The big theatres, the big opera houses, and the big venues would not in a million years accept small independent troupes like Nu Nu in their performance spaces on an equal footing with their own "mainstream" productions. How many independent artists/troupes have been allowed to perform their shows at the National? How many free tickets has the Royal Opera House offered to people on benefits or to people from outside London? It is indeed the state (of which artistic institutions are a part) that needs to create free(r) access to vocational education for people from marginalised communities and to give those people free access to the highest quality art (free tickets to the National, to the Royal Opera, to the RSC, etc.). Why can't the RSC come and perform for the poorest neighbourhoods in Bristol, free of charge? Why can't everybody benefit from the best productions of this world-renowned theatre company? One probably will not see Benedict Cumberbatch or Placido Domingo performing for the residents of a retirement home in London.

Whilst talking about diversity, the state preserves the status quo: inequality of access and participation to—most importantly—the arts infrastructure (not the artistic act). Why, as an independent theatre company in Bristol, can't Nu Nu perform one production per year in the Bristol Old Vic? That would provide us with the exposure to Old Vic's already established audiences and the wider public would be able to see what we create. The strategy for diversity (both in the case of *Song of Romania* and of the *Creative Case for Diversity*/public engagement)—if it wasn't just utopian—errs (?) by putting the cart before the horses and by (deliberately?) confusing what artists are expected to do and what governments and state institutions are expected to do. Society at large needs structural reform so that it can correctly incorporate its diversity. I argue that arts infrastructure and bureaucracy should become central to such reform. Unfortunately, that shift can never start from the artistic/creative act. Fair access should be given to all minorities and the marginalised (including artists) to mainstream venues, good schools, good theatre, great music, good healthcare, and fairly paid jobs. Artists should not be asked to engage with all sorts of disadvantaged communities, making projects that will remain implacably attached to the periphery in which they were created.

In the state's vision for diversity, arts organisations should turn into social hubs (just like the Communist Party wanted them to become laboratories for the study of communist doctrine) and artists into social workers whose aim is to support communities and wider society in rekindling their local economies. The aim is—in theory, evidently—that the artistic act achieves a rebalancing of social inequalities and brings marginalised communities to the centre of artistic life. That is simply an impossible task for the artist (for the professional one, in any case) to see through. Angela Gheorghiu—when rehearsing her *Tosca*—cannot be asked to salvage disadvantaged communities. Her role, her voice, and her act point to possible new compositions of sound and affect. Her voice and her art are liberating in themselves. The soprano will sing for any audience, but that audience needs to be de-marginalised and enabled to reach Gheorghiu, and that must be the task of the state, not of the artist.

ACE has recently revealed that it will now decide which projects to fund based on how relevant those projects are to audiences. As such, it will no longer be enough to produce high-quality work to receive funds. Simon Mellor (ACE's chief executive) says:

> Relevance is becoming the new litmus test. It will no longer be enough to produce high-quality work. You will need to be able to demonstrate that you are also facing all your stakeholders and communities in ways that they value. Large parts of the communities have lost all confidence in what they view as an out-of-touch establishment. Is the Arts Council viewed as part of the establishment? If so, how can trust be rebuilt? (Masso 2019)

Certainly not by distorting artists' instinct to reach for lives and people that are currently lacking, as Deleuze suggests. Evidently, arts and culture contain—in themselves—valuable seeds, directions, and propositions for balancing/alleviating inequalities and marginalisation, but to push art and the artist towards social work (in exchange for money) and into the neoliberal discourse of diversity is a grave reductionist exercise that favours only the petty calculations of funders, policymakers, the government, and the state.

4. The Artist's Role

William Deresiewicz (2015)—in his article *The Death of the Artist—And the Birth of the Creative Entrepreneur*—proposes an overview of how the artist has been perceived through the ages. Deresiewicz illustrates how the condition of the artist has shifted from genius to artisan/professional to artist-entrepreneur. Today, artists can no longer be seen as exceptional individuals who possess vision and inspiration—mysterious gifts received from above. In their present-day condition, artists are no longer solitary geniuses, or creators of cosmologies, magicians who tame and order the chaos to create—for the rest of us mortals—new imaginings of life. These magicians and prophets left us long ago: the sorcerer, possessor of a unique method (talent, gift, vocation?) for interpreting or experiencing the world/existence/chaos in the name of all the others has disappeared from today's stage. According to Deresiewicz, artists are no longer masters, professionals, or artisans either: they are no longer seen as possessors of strenuously accumulated wisdom in a certain discipline of art. The artist of today is no longer associated with ideas of individualism, originality, selfishness, and reclusion. Instead, the artist of today is a creative entrepreneur.

The language employed by ACE and the traumatic memories of *Song of Romania* convinced me to propose a fourth option for the artist of the twenty-first century: that of social worker and political activist by proxy. That is how ACE (and the state) seem to envisage the role of the today. In that direction, Goran Tomka's essay, *Escaping the Imaginary of Engaged Arts,* provides useful insights. Tomka uses the expression "activation of artists," which is, in my view, an apt way of suggesting the instrumentalisation of artists. Tomka (is it a coincidence that he too comes from Eastern Europe?) poses what I believe to be a fundamental question: "What is the activation good for? What cause does it serve?" (Tomka 2019:2).

What ACE does—conditional upon the release of funds—is to ask artist-recipients to activate themselves and provide a social service (subordinated to a neoliberal political thinking) in exchange for money received. Tomka comes with a pertinent explanation for such a strategy of barter imposed by the funder:

> At the foundation of it [activation] is the belief that communities are on their own …. To their aid, the arts should come. Arts organizations should turn into social hubs whose aim is to support communities and wider societies in rekindling their own local economies and finding patches to the broken health and education systems. (Tomka 2019:2)

In effect, ACE expects artists to make use of their skills and professional competencies/ talents to support less advantaged or marginalised communities. What is the aim? Certainly not that of proposing a new way of life and types of people who are lacking, but that of reigniting local economies. What happens in practice? The artist co-opts in the creative process people without a techne or skill in a particular artistic domain (public engagement is key). As in the case of *Song of Romania,* the effect is a diminution and dilution of the skill, an unfortunate mixing of competencies, resulting in ratatouille-like, pseudo-artistic acts. Surgeons cannot lend their scalpels to amateurs to cut into the organ, can they? None of us would like to be flown by non-pilots. Why do we assume that art is not like heart surgery or like flying planes and that it can afford a mixing of competencies and levels of skill?

Artistry (whether we choose to call ourselves artist-entrepreneurs or artist-seers) implies the existence of an inclination (a set of personal qualities) coupled with the emergence and expansion of techne, of method and competency, or of a sort of professionalization, a red line for composing chaos through affect, sensations, and precepts. This consistency of techne produces palpable effects (which are not necessarily and immediately relevant to a particular local community) of the deterritorialisation and composition of chaos towards possible lives and possible people. Van Gogh never healed the ills of his local community, but his work remains, oh, so relevant! If Nu Nu were to consult members of a certain community during the staging of *Hamlet,* for instance, we might not be able to elicit interesting opinions about the text or the characters because the themes that *Hamlet* deals with might not appear immediately or directly relevant to that particular community. That does not render the staging of *Hamlet* or the text itself irrelevant. The relevance for that community may appear delayed or mysterious and does not need to be explicated in the utilitarian, urgent terms laid out by ACE. The economic effects might also appear delayed, but they nevertheless will appear. To want to know whom a particular theatre project will help here and now is another way of dismissing the value of creation and regimenting the artist in the register of exchange values controlled by the funder.

By asking me to put the problems of the community before my own concerns, obsessions, passions, and psychoses regarding *Hamlet* (be they as random and detached as possible), ACE asks me to help it deliver something akin to community and social work and ultimately politically motivated work. But that cannot be the primary role of the artist, because, as noted before:

> Issues that produce social, economic, and moral deprivations cannot be solved by arts, creative industries, or whatever we come to call them next. They should and can be solved with meaningful social and economic measures. (Tomka 2019:3)

Tomka continues by pointing out that:

> The best arts and culture can do is to mask social-economic inequalities by having people from diverse backgrounds participate in local cultural life. If we accept that game, we are not alleviating troubles but relieving responsibilities. (Tomka 2019:3)

In ACE's public engagement/relevance requirements and *Creative Case for Diversity,* arts and culture are seen as a facile solution to deeply ingrained socioeconomic problems:

> Arts are increasingly seen as a cleansing solution. Don't worry about that bloody stain, that social divide, that urban deprivation—just throw a brand-new arts centre and your social fabric will be as good as new! (Tomka 2019:3)

An experiment on *Hamlet* can never be reduced to disenfranchised communities or marginalised people or to the lack of access to education or jobs. Entwining socioeconomic problems (which evidently points to a sort of political activism) of a given community with the moral dilemmas in *Hamlet* is diminishing the amplitude and the breath of the dramatic text. It is detrimental to turn a staging of *Hamlet* into a debate on social, economic, or political issues, as important as those issues might be. ACE demands that untrained people or non-artists become co-creators of artistic acts, in a similar way to how the Communist Party wanted to force the multilaterally developed new man out of the basic condition of creator of agricultural or industrial goods. Let's remember the communists' advice: "Professional artistic institutions grant qualified support to amateur artists collaborating with them in order to increase the qualitative level of the performance" (Scînteia 1976:1). The idea that artists can be anything you want them to be is utterly false. According to van Houte (2019:5), "not every artist is a social artist." I argue that no artist is a social artist and whoever is a social artist is not fully an artist. The artist's role is to shout, to suffer, to never be content, to tell unpalatable truths, to be the king's fool. The artist cannot be a politician or a social worker, but someone who primarily points to possible life and possible people. No one should ask artists (in exchange for money or whatever else) to automatically engage with the wider public or to ensure diversity by all means in their work. In the same way, artists cannot and should not be required to engage with birds, ugliness, old age, blonde ladies, or the colour purple. The artistic act is the result of the artist living through and consuming a unique, individual experience, albeit emerging from within a given community and in a given political context, which overshoots into a possible, new world. The artistic act cannot be anticipated nor programmed towards any desired outcomes.

5. Conclusion

Isolation, solitude, madness, stubbornness, foolishness, and uselessness in concert with the day's social or political priorities should be praised; the moving askew from so-called relevance measured against the immediate, concrete, and next-minute wishes and needs of a community should not be dismissed as unproductive. These are key to the artist's ability to point towards imagined worlds, towards better, different, and not-yet-existing types of people and ways of life. Guattari's value of creation (an effect of what I have defined as artistic freedom) differentiates—in a definitive way—arts from the social and political activities and theoretical discourse from praxis. Art must remain a bed for the flowing river of our inner lives, which are not made only of economic, social, and political needs. Art is also not a festival, nor a celebration. Art fulfils other, different functions: it contests, by opposing its possible life and possible people to current states of affairs. In order to achieve valid possible worlds, artists must be allowed to choose their own path. The aspect that both regimes (communist and capitalist/neoliberal) overlook is that art must necessarily puncture through the political, social, and economic givens. Art must not be put under the control of theoretical discourse, but be allowed to produce new discursivity as an effect of praxis.

I note that in similar fashion to *Song of Romania*, ACE's petty (commercially motivated) dealings with artists appear rather primitive and short-sighted. I have read a number of official reports about the role of arts in British society. All those reports talked about the arts and creative industries in terms of contribution to GDP. The Office for National Statistics' report for 2018 shows that "the arts and culture industry has grown £390 million in a year and now contributes £10.8 billion a year to the UK economy" (ACE 2019). That suggests that arts are regarded as primarily a moneymaking activity. No reports seem to be concerned with a new way of life or the new life and new people that artists propose. By pulling artistic praxis into a socio-political and economic type of discourse, art is forced to abandon its role of illuminating new possibilities. It might indeed bring more money to the state coffers, but to a great degree, it stops being art and functions just like any other industry.

Returning to Blandiana, who talks about poets not being allowed to become the makers of our world, I add that if artists were funded to freely dream about their projects and ideas, there would be a guaranteed increase in diversity and an abundance of relevance of their artistic acts: "Had it been created by the poets, our world would have looked radically different" (Blandiana 2016). ACE should give money to marginalised people to go and see the best opera, theatre, and music shows produced and performed by the best artists. That would materially change the lives of marginalised people and inspire them to become true artists themselves (those ones who truly possess an inclination). ACE should encourage the big arts institutions and educational/vocational establishments to open their doors generously (not just in the name of the box ticking) to less well-known artists (of great potential) from marginalised communities. ACE should pay both big venues and less well-known artists to take risks and fail. That would trigger a true diversification of the arts and automatically augment the relevance of arts for everybody.

To conclude, I note that it is possible that my paranoid eye masks the immigrant artist's insufficient understanding of the philosophy behind the funder's strategy. It may be possible that my feelings are the result of an improper, incomplete understanding of the more intricate ethical and historical/cultural implications and explications for the funder's strategy. An example in that direction could be the UK's class system and the way it has historically operated in the arts: a chronic lack of opportunity to engage with the arts that UK's marginalised community members have experienced through the ages. Perhaps the ACE strategy—although eminently theoretical, as I have argued— is producing its desired effects. However, the BAFTA awards of 2020 did not illustrate that, as there were no black/BME artists nominated in any category. The latest report on diversity in the arts institutions in England shows the following: "a slight rise in the BME workforce (from 12% to 14%) ... only 5% of staff at major museums are non-white ... disabled workers across the national portfolio has risen from 4% to 5% (despite 20% of adults identified as having a work-limiting disability) ... the female workforce in the national portfolio has fallen from 55% in 2015 to 50% in 2028" (Brown, 2019).

Perhaps ACE's strategy needs more time ... perhaps it will work ... perhaps it's just me and my inescapable paranoia.

REFERENCES

Arendt, Hannah. (1998) *The Human Condition (2nd ed.). Chicago, IL: University of Chicago Press.*

Arts Council England. (2019) Contribution of the Arts and Culture Industry to the UK economy, <https://www.artscouncil.org.uk/publication/contribution-arts-and-culture-industry-uk-economy-0>. *(Accessed 31 October 2019).*

Bălaşa, Sabin. (1975) Creatia Artistica—Un Permanent Examen in Fata Propriului Popor (Artistic Creation—A Permanent Exam in Front of One Own's Nation). *Scînteia,* June 13.

Blandiana, Ana. (2016) Istoria ca Viitor. <https://s3-eu-central-1.amazonaws.com/pressone/wp-content/uploads/2016/03/24175425/Discursul-Anei-Blandiana-de-acceptare-a-DHC-UBB-Cluj.pdf> (Accessed 31 October 2019).

Brown, Mark. (2019) English Art Bodies Slow to Become More Diverse, Report Shows. <https://www.theguardian.com/culture/2019/feb/12/english-arts-bodies-slow-to-become-more-diverse-report-shows> (Accessed 31 October 2019)

Ceausescu, Nicolae. (1976) *Congresul Educatiei Politice si al Culturii Socialiste 2-4 Iunie 1976 (The Congress of Political Education and Socialist Culture 2-4 June 1976).* Bucharest: Editura Politica.

Deleuze, Gilles. (2007) From A to Z. DVD. Directed by Pierre-Andre Boutang. Los Angeles, CA: Semiotexte.

Deleuze, Gilles and Felix Guattari. (1994) *What is Philosophy?* Translated by Hugh Tomlinson and Graham Burchell. New York, NY: Columbia University Press.

Deresiewicz, William. (2015) The Death of the Artist—And the Birth of the Creative Entrepreneur. *The Atlantic,* January/February. <https://www.theatlantic.com/magazine/archive/2015/01/the-death-of-the-artist-and-the-birth-of-the-creative-entrepreneur/383497/> (Accessed 31 October 2019).

Gardner, Lyn. (2019) Rethinking the Purpose of British Arts Institutions. *Howlround Theatre Commons,* 17 February. <https://howlround.com/rethinking-purpose-british-arts-institutions> (Accessed 31 October 2019).

Guattari, Felix. (2015) *Machinic Eros: Writings on Japan,* Gary Genosko and Jay Hetrick (eds.). Minneapolis: Univocal.

Ionesco, Eugene. (1992) *Note si Contranote*. Bucuresti: Humanitas.

Ionesco, Eugene. (1993) *Prezent Trecut Trecut Prezent*. Bucuresti: Humanitas.

Jacobsen, Ushma Chauhan. (2018) Languaging in Art and Cultural Management. *Arts Management Quarterly* 128: 17–22.

Liepins, Maija. (2019) CAS Presents: How to Apply for Arts Council England Funding. *Chapelartsstudios*, January 23 <http://www.chapelartsstudios.co.uk/blog/cas-support/cas-presents-how-to-apply-for-arts-council-england-funding/> (Accessed 31 October 2019).

Mahamdallie, Hassan. (2012) What is the Case for Diversity. *People Dancing: The Foundation for Community Dance*. <https://www.communitydance.org.uk/DB/animated-library/what-is-the-creative-case-for-diversity?ed=27830> (Accessed 31 October 2019).

Masso, Giverny. (2019) Arts Council: Relevance not Excellence will be New Litmus Test for Funding. *The Stage*, April 8. <https://www.thestage.co.uk/news/2019/arts-council-relevance-not-excellence-will-be-new-litmus-test-for-funding/> (Accessed 31 October 2019).

Nwonka, Clive. (2019) The Arts were Supposed to Champion Diversity. What Went Wrong? *The Guardian*, February 15 <https://www.theguardian.com/commentis-free/2019/feb/15/arts-diversity-arts-council-england-inequality>(Accessed 31 October 2019).

Scînteia. (1976) Festivalul National al Educatiei si Culturii Socialiste "Cântarea României, Stralucita Manifestare a Dragostei de Munca, a Virtutilor Creatoare ale Poporului Nostru, Expresie a Democratismului Politicii Culturale a Partidului Comunist Român (The National Festival Of Socialist Education and Culture, Brilliant Expression of the Love for Work, of the Creative Virtues of Our People, Expression of the Democratization of the Cultural Politics of the Romanian Communist Party). *Scînteia*, November 28.

Shishkova, Vassilika. (2019a) Everyday Creators: Friends or Foes? Report from the IETM Plenary Meeting, 28-31 March 2019. *IETM Inclusion*, April 13 <https://www.ietm.org/en/themes/article/everyday-creators-friends-or-foes> (Accessed 31 October 2019).

Shishkova, Vassilika. (2019b) If Funders Really Wanted to Support Artists, What could They Do? Report from the IETM Plenary Meeting, 28-31 March 2019. *IETM Themes*, April 14, <https://www.ietm.org/en/themes/article/if-funders-really-wanted-to-support-artists-what-could-they-do> (Accessed 31 October 2019).

Tomka, Goran. (2019) Escaping the Imaginary of Engaged Arts. *IETM Inclusion*, March

22 <https://www.ietm.org/en/themes/article/escaping-the-imaginary-of-engaged-arts> (Accessed 31 October 2019).

Unlimited. (2016) The Creative Case for Diversity: A Beginners' Guide by a Beginner. *Weareunited,* June 7 <https://weareunlimited.org.uk/the-creative-case-for-diversity-a-beginners-guide-by-a-beginner/> (Accessed 31 October 2019).

van Houte, Nan. (2019) Should Our Funds for the Arts Pay for Cultural Democracy? *IETM Inclusion,* March 18. <https://www.ietm.org/en/themes/article/should-our-funds-for-the-arts-pay-for-cultural-democracy> (Accessed 31 October 2019).

Young Eugene B., Gary Genosko, and Janell Watson. (2013) *The Deleuze and Guattari Dictionary.* London, New Delhi, New York, Sydney: Bloomsbury.

EMPOWERMENT AND DIGITIZATION IN ARTS MANAGEMENT EDUCATION: A CRITICAL SELF-REFLECTION OF A 'WESTERN' EDUCATOR

RAPHAELA HENZE

Heilbronn University

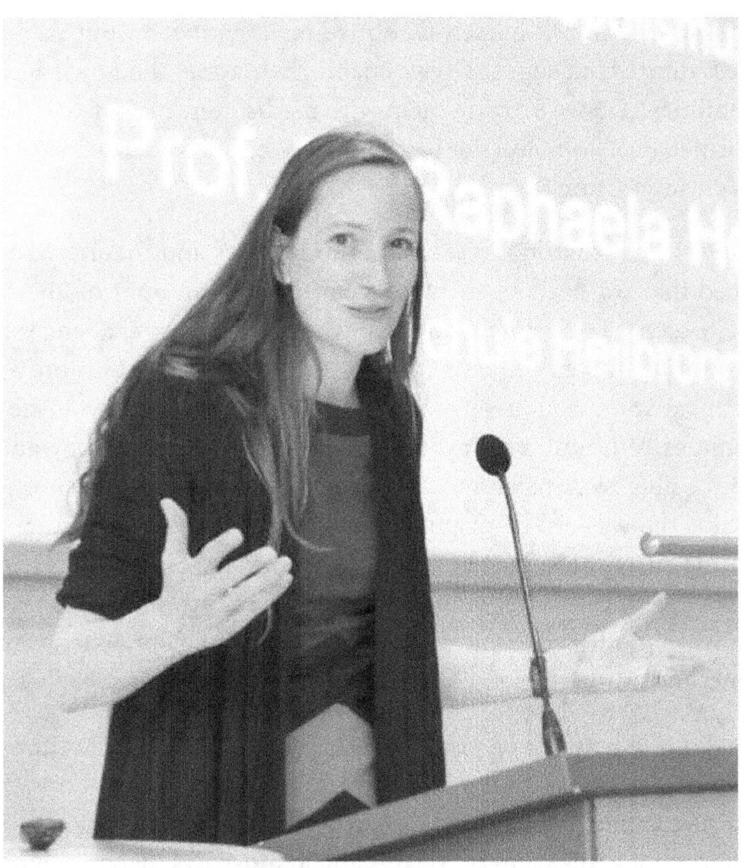

Raphaela Henze is professor of Arts and Cultural Management at Heilbronn University and Co-Investigator of the Arts & Humanities Research Council funded, international and interdisciplinary network Brokering Intercultural Exchange (www.managingculture.net). Prior to joining Heilbronn University in 2010 Raphaela Henze worked in several senior management positions in universities, ministries, and foundations. Her main research focus is on the impacts of globalization and internationalization on arts management and arts management education as well as on the role of arts and culture in times of rising populism.

For more than nine years, as I educate aspiring arts managers, I critically self-reflect on the impact I can make on the generation of my students. There is a lot of talk and literature about empowerment these days—particularly in the context of participatory arts projects and in intercultural arts management (Canas 2015; Fernández Carrasco et al. 2016; Henze 2018; Matarasso 2019; McHenry and Annwar 2011) – but not so when it comes to the education of arts management students (Durrer 2019; Saha 2013). This is a huge shortcoming, which needs to be addressed.

As educators, we have to ask ourselves: do we really empower our students to courageously address future challenges? Do we enable them to set their own agendas and take over responsibilities? Do we provide them with media literacy, which will allow them to take well-informed decisions and not be prone to believe fake news and propaganda? Or do we just teach and lecture them?

I am not saying that it is wrong to teach methodologies and theories. To the contrary, I am convinced that we need them more than the vast amount of "best practices" in our discipline, which will definitely not help when addressing challenges that appear in different and more complex contexts (Mattocks 2017). This is also one of the reasons that I am sceptical about the involvement of practitioners directly at the beginning of study programmes. Without a sound understanding of methodology and theory, students will not be able to transfer and apply their knowledge. Without knowing epistemologies outside the western hemisphere, they will be ignorant of new approaches that might help tackle current challenges at home and abroad (Henze 2019). I assume most educators will agree to this—but let us self-critically reflect on what we really do in our programmes. Is what our curriculae demand us to do sufficient, when we look closer at the current and upcoming challenges that arts managers will most likely face?

Within this text, I briefly touch on populism, protection of cultural heritage, internationalisation, and globalisation, as I consider these topics most urgent, notwithstanding the ones that will surely emerge and that I am unfortunately unable to foresee. I then focus on media literacy, since this seems to be missing in most arts management programmes, even though it is a key competence. Finally, the conclusion offers first ideas on what we as educators can do in order to help to empower aspiring arts managers.

POPULISM

The topic of populism is not a new one. For decades, we have experienced left-wing populism in South and Central America (in several countries, e.g., Brazil and Argentina, this is now shifting to the right, with a particularly dangerous and frightening situation in Venezuela). We know the reactions from the art world to this by Augusto Boal's Theatre of the Oppressed,[1] for instance. I question whether we as educators have learned

---

1 Simplified Theatre of The Oppressed is a theatrical format coined by Brazilian artist Augusto Boal in

enough lessons from the experiences of colleagues in academia and practice outside the western hemisphere. Putting Paulo Freire's seminal work "Pedagogy of the Oppressed" on students' literature lists seems like a good beginning, but it is not yet enough. We have seen the election of Donald Trump and a highly xenophobic Brexit campaign that unfortunately proved successful in the end—interestingly, this came as a surprise to many arts managers in the UK (Henze 2017, 35). We have seen Marine le Pen almost become the president of France and the rise of many other right-wing populists all around Europe.

That populism threatens a free artistic scene and cultural rights is a fact. In Europe, it leads to self-censorship of cultural programmes and institutions. The attacks on artistic freedom have not been properly sanctioned by politicians and governments, which do not want to confront an electoral body that is shifting to the right (Dragićević Šešić and Nikolić 2019, 33f). Despite the official UNESCO avowal to support the plurality of expression and alternative forms of art (UNESCO Convention 2005), what we experience today speaks a different language (Dragićević Šešić and Nikolić 2019, 34).

Where are the role models in our discipline that take responsibility and raise their voices against all forms of oppression? I am not saying that they are not there. I know that equity and social justice education is something that colleagues, particularly in the US, advocate for. However, it is—again—not yet enough. Even huge networks like the European Network on Cultural Management and Policy (ENCATC) or the American Association of Arts Administration Educators (AAAE) are relatively hesitant when it comes to taking a clear stand on political issues, although several of their members are involved in or teach cultural policy.

Protection of Cultural Heritage

During the EU Year of Cultural Heritage in 2018, it became even more apparent that in many parts of the world the danger in which cultural heritage finds itself in is tremendous. As Shohat and Stam (1994, 183) wrote more than twenty-five years ago: "Arts and culture are symbolic battlegrounds." It is not only about passion and emotions, but also about power and the prerogative of interpretation. Arts and culture are never neutral (Henze 2017, 24). This can be demonstrated by the manner in which the Islamic State treats cultural heritage.

The destructions are meant to send a message to the Christian, western world, negating tradition and history in a senseless and brutal way (Henze 2017, 24). This applies for the destruction of Nineveh, Iraq, or the Buddha statutes of Bamiyan, Afghanistan back in 2001, which was one of the first examples of global communication being used to enhance the impact of the destruction of cultural heritage (Smith 2015, 38).

---

the 1970ies. Theatre is understood as a means for social and political change particularly by strong audience involvement and community engagement.

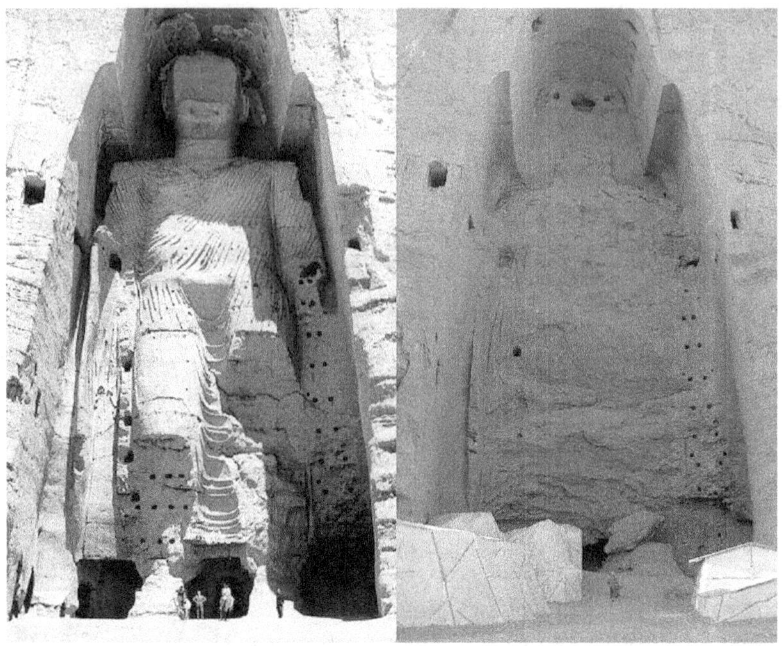

Figure 1: Buddha statues in Bamiyan (Wikipedia).

These are deliberate attacks on cultural identities. The battlefield is, therefore, no longer symbolic but all-too-tragically real. All these hate messages and videos of destructions —called "socially mediated terrorism" by Smith at al. (2016, 1)—are spread around the world online for propaganda purposes. The Taliban's use of media communication was from the beginning highly sophisticated and flexible. The internet has provided the fastest and most effective propaganda tool for them. They have their own, attractively designed websites, where all data is provided in five languages. If one website gets closed down by the CIA, for instance, they just open up a new one (Smith 2015).

We have also seen the reactions to this by the experts of digital archaeology in the form of a 3D replica of the 1,800-year-old arch of triumph from Palmyra. We can argue with Walter Benjamin and lament that the aura is missing, and it is. However, we could approach it in the way one of my students recently did. While the replica is obviously not the real one, it is now part of the history of Palmyra. We cannot deny the senseless destruction; it forms part of the history of the city. We have to deal with it, try to react to it, and the next chapter in the century-long history might now come out of a 3D printer.

Internationalisation and Globalisation

According to an empirical study of more than 350 arts managers from different cultural organisations and institutions from forty-six different countries, the majority considers their work to be international (Henze 2017). It is important to stress that these were not arts managers working in international contexts per se—e.g., for the Goethe Institut, the British Council, or huge funding bodies. Participants were working in the city theatre in

Plymouth, a museum in Cape Town, or an orchestra in Berlin, for instance. Do we really prepare our students for these international and maybe even more so intercultural work environments? This is a huge topic that definitely needs to form part of our curriculae, and it definitely goes far beyond language skills and intercultural competencies (Durrer 2019).

In many of our study programmes' rules and regulations, we find claims like this one, which was randomly picked from one of the many cultural management programmes in Germany:

> § 2 (4) 1 the goal of the master programme in arts management is: **to enable our alumni to react creatively and competently to the current challenges arts organisations are facing.**

This sounds good, right?

It is not sufficient. It is about reacting. Our discipline merely reacts and does not innovate enough. Constance DeVereaux (2009) hinted at this a long time ago already. It is about current challenges (or about those topics that we thought important when implementing the programmes)—what about the ones we do not yet foresee? I assume that we will face issues concerning, for instance, fake news and propaganda spread by terrorists and populists alike. There will be more "sophisticated" ways of destroying cultural heritage, more ways to attack identities, and more ways to infiltrate even larger parts of societies with right-wing thoughts that we are unable to fathom today; digitization will play a central role in all of this. Migration, globalisation and climate change (Figueira and Fullman 2019: 319 f.) will most likely provide us with more challenges than they do already and require new forms of collaboration. Change and transformation will be our constant companions. Are we prepared for this in a discipline that finds itself spending a lot of time and effort on defending century-old institutions?

MEDIA LITERACY

There are many new thoughts, ideas, experimental formats, and courage that will better prepare students for a work environment that is relatively alien to many of those teaching them today. Among many other things, such as network competencies, language skills, a sound knowledge of a variety of different narratives and methodologies, and the ability for critical self-reflection, I argue for media literacy that is, to the best of my knowledge, embedded in only a very few arts management programs.

According to the National Association for Media Literacy Education in the US, media literacy is "The ability to access, analyse, evaluate, create, and act using all forms of communication." There are several aspects in this definition that will be important to (aspiring) arts managers.

Use of Digital Media

There is a wealth of literature on how to use social media marketing for cultural organisations or audience development, for instance. Eight years ago, I conducted a survey on the use of social media in German theatres (Henze 2011). Re-reading it today, I figure that cultural organisations have come a long way.

Just one random example of what arts institutions do is a joint project between Europeana and Culture24: VanGoYourself, which is a website that encourages people to mimic a range of famous Van Gogh paintings. Users find a painting they like from the VanGoYourself website, copy the pose and take a selfie, which they then upload.

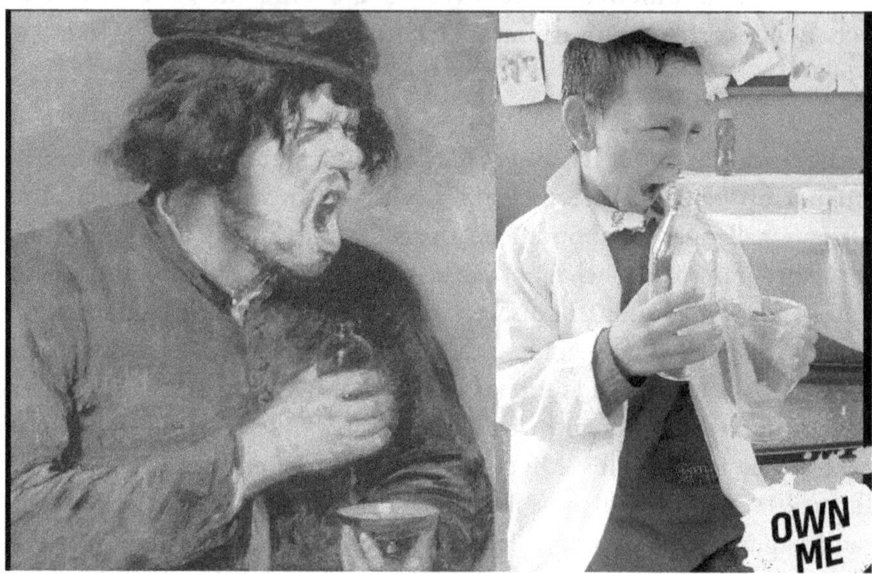

Figure 2: https://vangoyourself.com/vango/aci-iksiri-adriaen-
brouwer-1605-06-1638-vangod-by-burcu-2/.

The site won several awards in 2015. It is considered to be a good way of getting the audience interested in particular artworks and has an obvious viral element to it.

There is definitely a lot more that could be presented here to show that cultural organizations can put media to good use, particularly when it comes to audience development, outreach, and archiving.

Creation of Digital Tools

Things get more complex when it comes to creation. We could argue that the creation is up to specialists and experts—and this is particularly true when it comes to games or special effects. However, I have a strong feeling that our students will have to be able to develop an app one day and thus must have some ideas about how to code. In the closing chapter of his book, *The End of Education,* Neal Postman (1995) reminds us that "technology education is not a technical subject. It is a branch of the humanities" (191). Did anybody think of this when designing arts management curriculae?

Nevertheless, there surely has been quite a lot of development in the sector—unfortunately not so much in education.

Just to give an example of how the rise of digital technology has helped generalize the process of buying a piece of art that was previously monopolized by auction houses' regular customers. Online marketplaces selling affordable artworks are popping up and reshaping the rules of offer and demand. Thousands of unknown artists now have access to an online market, taking care of all of the buying and promoting processes. This is praised as a kind of democratisation, because it helps to get around gatekeepers like curators. Others say that it is exactly this that blurs the line and that quality needs the protection of experts.

The arts change because of this "digital turn"—new art forms emerge that we have to familiarize ourselves with. My students just recently presented an artist they find interesting and who "paints" with his smart phone.

Rembrandt is coming out of the printer; music is composed by artificial intelligence.

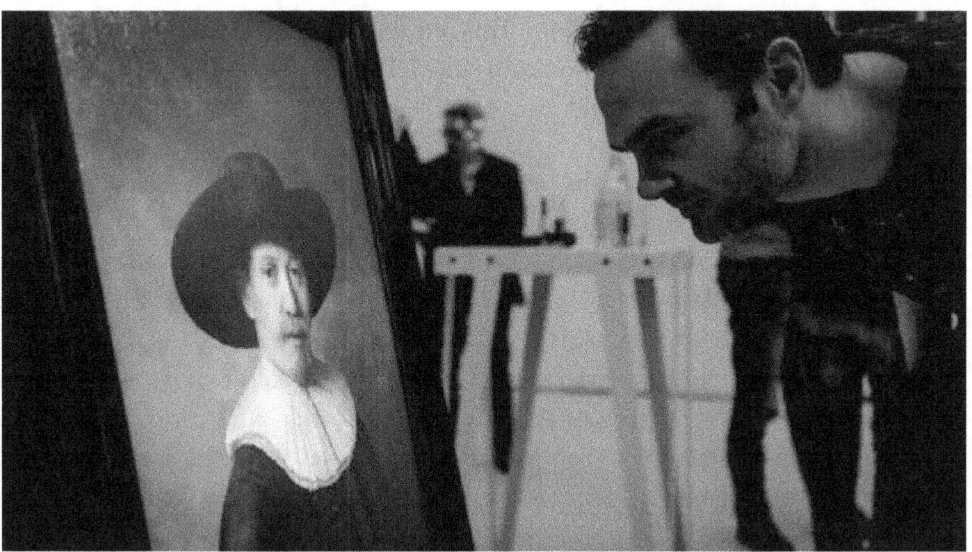

Figure 3: (dpa/picture alliance/ANP/Robin van Lonkhuijsen).

Ability to Access and Evaluate Information

At the centre of what media literacy in arts management education should be is the ability to access and evaluate information. We are aware that many people in the world are not able to access all information available online, e.g., colleagues in China or Kashmir. Cutting people off from information can be a very powerful tool to oppress them.

Accessibility is a right that we should fight for and we should ensure that all people have an opportunity to gather information from a variety of sources. However, it is exactly this variety of resources that we need to address and that should be at the heart of media literacy education. I believe that being correctly informed/having a sound and reliable knowledge base is key for whatever you do.

Conclusion

Even being from a different generation, not being a digital native, and only having had limited experiences concerning (im)migration, there are things we as educators can do:

1) Be aware of the danger of the single story. The Nigerian author Chimamanda Ngozi Adichie, in her amazing Ted talk (https://www.ted.com/talks/chimam anda_adichie_the_danger_of_a_single_story), brings this to the point. We are accomplices to the single story that is told in European/western arts management courses. It is almost entirely a western story. We need to give students an opportunity to experience other narratives, methodologies, and epistemologies. This requires that we actively seek partners in countries and regions that have been marginalized in our discourses for too long (Henze 2019), which is not an easy task (Durrer and Henze 2018, 3). We need more literature from authors outside the western hemisphere. This requires more effort and money for translations. Free online translation tools like Deepl can have a huge impact and put artificial intelligence to good use.

2) Talk to people involved. This is only possible when you have a network—and this would lead me on another journey on the importance of networks in cultural management on which I am most happy to embark in another text. However, contacting people from the respective regions is important when we strive to overcome our ethnocentric frames of reference (Henze 2019). Networks like Brokering Intercultural Exchange (www.managingculture.net), which are not only open for researchers, but also for students and Ph.D. candidates, can help overcome the dependency on unreliable media resources by providing reliable contacts and forums to gather and exchange personally and virtually.

3) Train students to constantly question the information they receive. There is an enormous amount of literature on propaganda. Do we make use of this in arts management education? Do our students know the propaganda model by Chomsky? I think they should.

4) We need more open access resources like this journal. The "publish or perish" doctrine in academia makes us accept standards that we would not necessarily accept in any other area of life. Making more texts available to the public via

open access does not have to result in lower quality. It is partly on us to have sound but fair and objective peer reviews for open source journals.

5) We need to overcome our hostility towards technology that seems to be embedded in our discipline and that might even reach back to Benjamin and Adorno. There is a lot to be sceptical or even afraid of when it comes to technology, but abstaining from it and hoping it will pass us by is not an option. It is on us or our students to use these tools to our advantage and we have to train them in media literacy. At German universities, artificial intelligence is the next big thing. A lot of research funding goes into it. Why not join forces? I am convinced that arts management can profit from it.

6) Last, but not least, we as educators have to be particularly aware of our responsibilities and those of public intellectuals (Modood 2019). When I watched TV in my childhood, there was usually at least one respected person from the cultural sector or arts scene present at talk shows or political debates. These people have more or less completely disappeared from the public scene and media. In Germany, not enough[2] artists or intellectual raise their voices to point out inequities, even though they are living in a country where doing this would not put them in danger. When the ever-present Kardashians are the benchmark, we are in deep trouble!

WORKS CITED

Canas, Tania. 2015. "10 Things You Need to Consider if You are an Artist – Not of the Refugee and Asylum Seeker Community – Looking to Work with our Community." *Rise Refugee,* http://riserefugee.org/10-things-you-need-to-consider-if-you-are-an-artist-not-of-the-refugee-and-asylum-seeker-community-looking-to-work-with-our-community/#.

DeVereaux, Constance. 2009. "Cultural Management and the Discourse of Practice." In *Jahrbuch für Kulturmanagement,* 155–67. Bielefeld: Transcript Verlag.

Dragićević Šešić, Milena and Mirjana Nikolić. 2019. *Situating Populist Politics: Arts & Media Nexus.* Belgrade: Clio.

Durrer, Victoria, and Raphaela Henze. 2018. "Leaving Comfort Zones." *Arts Management Quarterly, Leaving Comfort Zones. Cultural Inequalities* 129 (June): 3.

---

2   A relatively recent development in the German arts sector has been the "Declaration of the Many," https://www.dievielen.de/multilingual.

Durrer, Victoria. 2019. "A Call for Reflexivity: Implications of the Internationalisation Agenda for Arts Management Programmes within Higher Education." In Managing Culture: Reflecting on Exchange in Global Times, 171–203. Edited by Victoria Durrer and Raphaela Henze. Cham: Palgrave MacMillan.

Fernández Carrasco, Ruben, Moisés Carmona Monferrer, and Andres Di Masso Tarditi. 2016. "Exploring Links between Empowerment and Community-Based Arts and Cultural Practices: Perspectives from Barcelona Practitioners." *International Journal of Inclusive Education* 20 (3): 229–45. https://doi.org/10.1080/13603116.2015.10 47659.

Figueira, Carla, and Aimee Fullman. 2019. "Rethinking Cultural Relations and Exchange in the Critical Zone." In *Managing Culture: Reflecting on Exchange in Global Times*. Edited by Victoria Durrer and Raphaela Henze, . 319–339 Cham: Palgrave Macmillan

Henze, Raphaela. 2011. "Nutzung des Web 2.0 an deutschen Theatern und Schauspielhäusern." In *Jahrbuch für Kulturpolitik*, 219–230. Essen: Klartext Verlag.

———. 2017. *Introduction to International Arts Management.* Wiesbaden: Springer.

———.2018. "The Master's Tool will never Dismantle the Master's House." *Arts Management Quarterly, Leaving Comfort Zones. Cultural Inequalities* 129 (June): 29–35.

———. 2019. "More than Just Lost in Translation. The Ethnocentrism of our Frames of Reference." In *Managing Culture: Reflecting on Exchange in Global Times*. Edited by Victoria Durrer and Raphaela Henze, 51–80.Cham: Palgrave Macmillan.

Matarasso, Francois. 2019. *A Restless Art.* Calouste Gulbenikan Foundation.

Mattocks, Kate. 2017. "Just Describing is not Enough: Policy Learning, Transfer, and the Limits of Best Practices." *The Journal of Arts Management, Law, and Society* 48 (2): 85–97.

McHenry and Julia Annwar. 2011. "Rural Empowerment through the Arts: The Role of the Arts in Civic and Social Participation in the Mid West region of Western Australia." *Journal of Rural Studies* 27 (3): 245–53.

Modood, Tariq. 2019. "Thinking about Public Intellectuals." *Journal of the Society for Contemporary Thought and the Islamicate World.* https://sctiw.org/wp-content/uploads/2019/01/171-Public-Intellectuals-in-the-Global-Arena-Tariq-Modood.pdf.

Postman, Neil. 1995. *The End of Education.* Random House: New York.

Saha, Anamik. 2013. "The Cultural Industries in a Critical Multicultural Pedagogy." In *Cultural Work and Higher Education.* Edited by Daniel Ashton and Caitriona Noonan, 214–31. Basingstroke: Palgrave Macmillan.

Shohat, Ella, and Robert Stam. 1994. *Unthinking Eurocentrism*. New York: Routledge.

Smith, Claire. 2015. *Social Media and the Destruction of World Heritage as Global Propaganda*. https://eprints.ucm.es/35077/1/Conferenciainaugural.pdf.

Smith, Claire, Heather Burke, Cherrie de Leiuen, and Gary Jackson. 2016. "The Islamic State's Symbolic War: Da'esh's Socially Mediated Terrorism as a Threat to Cultural Heritage." *Journal of Social Archeology* 16 (2): 164–80.

WHOSE GOVERNANCE, WHOSE GOOD? CULTURAL POLICY AND GOVERNANCE IN THE PHILIPPINES

JASON VITORILLO

LASALLE College of the Arts

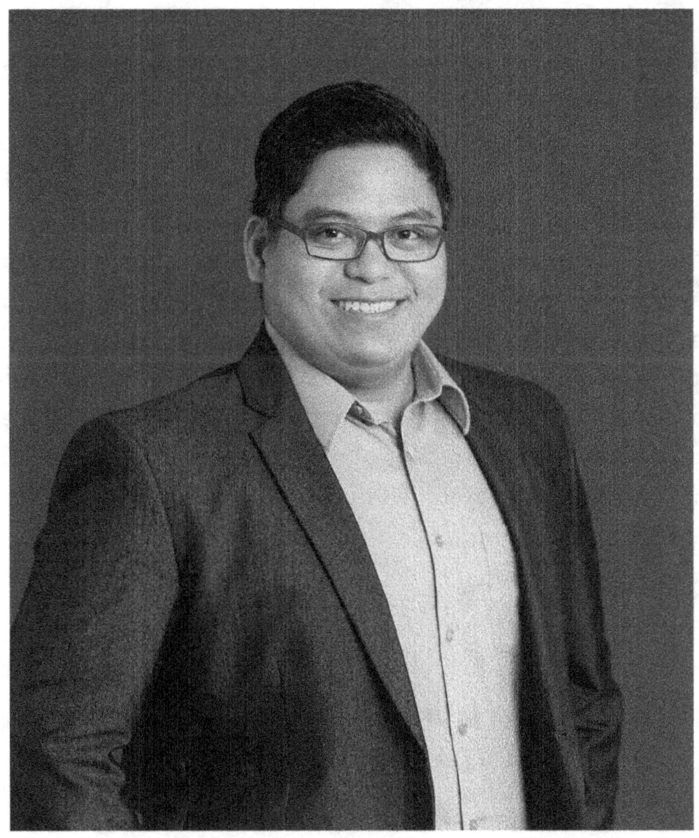

Jason Vitorillo has been in the academe for over ten years, and was previously the Program Chair of the Arts Management Program of the School of Design and Arts, College of Saint Benilde in Manila. He is currently teaching at and is the Lecturer-in-Charge of the BA(Hons) Arts Management Programme of LASALLE College of the Arts, Singapore. His research interests include international cultural policy, models of arts funding, audience development and engagement, arts and cultural management education, and intangible cultural heritage of indigenous communities.

ABSTRACT

A few months ago, I chanced upon the book on *Cultural Democracy: The Arts, Community, and the Public Purpose* by James Bau Graves, and was struck by the question he posed in his introduction: "What does your community need to keep its culture vital and meaningful?" This question made me reflect on my interest in intangible cultural heritage management and cultural policy, and the current conditions in the Philippines. In 2001, while I was still studying to be a dancer and thespian, I was intrigued by the cultures and artistic expressions of Indigenous people in the Philippines. I visited a couple of Indigenous communities in the Central and Southern Philippines. I watched their dances, listened to their songs, and noted their stories often asking questions on why and how they came about with what I just experienced. A few years following this immersion, I started on a research project on nurturing Indigenous culture and arts in the Philippines, taking a closer look at how the National Commission for Culture and the Arts (NCCA) in the Philippines formulated policies and created mechanisms to provide Indigenous people with the support they need to keep their cultures alive. This has been a constant inquiry of mine ever since. How have the policies and mechanisms developed in the past decade? Is it responsive to the needs of the communities?

Keywords: Theatre, public engagement, diversity

¿EL GOBIERNO DE QUIÉN, EL BIEN DE QUIÉN? POLÍTICA CULTURAL Y GOBERNANZA EN FILIPINAS

RESUMEN

Hace unos meses, me topé con el libro sobre Democracia cultural: las artes, la comunidad y el propósito público de James Bau Graves, y me llamó la atención la pregunta que planteó en su introducción: "¿Qué necesita su comunidad para mantener su cultura? ¿vital y significativo? Esta pregunta me hizo reflexionar sobre mi interés en la gestión del patrimonio cultural inmaterial y la política cultural, y las condiciones actuales en Filipinas. En 2001, mientras aún estudiaba para ser bailarín y actor, me intrigaban las culturas y las expresiones artísticas de los pueblos indígenas en Filipinas. Visité un par de comunidades indígenas en el centro y sur de Filipinas. Vi sus bailes, escuché sus canciones y noté sus historias a menudo haciendo preguntas sobre por qué y cómo surgieron con lo que acabo de experimentar. Unos años después de esta inmersión, comencé un proyecto de investigación sobre el fomento de la cultura y las artes indígenas en Filipinas, analizando más de cerca cómo la Comisión Nacional de Cultura y Artes (NCCA) en Filipinas formuló políticas y creó mecanismos para proporcionar Pueblos indígenas con el apoyo que necesitan para mantener vivas sus culturas. Esta ha sido una constante investigación mía desde entonces. ¿Cómo se han desarrollado las políticas y los mecanismos en la última década? ¿Responde a las necesidades de las comunidades?

Palabras clave: Teatro, compromiso público, diversidad

谁的治理，谁的利益？菲律宾文化政策与治理

摘要

几个月前，我偶然阅读了James Bau Graves的著作《文化民主：艺术、社区与公共目的》，我被他在导论中提出的疑问所震惊："你的社区需要什么来保持其文化活力与意义？"。这个问题使我反思我对非物质文化遗产管理与文化政策的兴趣，以及菲律宾当前的情况。2001年，当我还在学习成为一名舞者和演员时，我被菲律宾土著人民的文化和艺术表现所吸引。我拜访了菲律宾中南部的两个土著人民社区。我观看了他们的舞蹈，聆听他们的歌曲，同时发现他们的故事经常会发出有关故事为何以及如何发生的疑问。对此痴迷几年后，我开始进行一项有关于在菲律宾培养土著人民文化与艺术的研究课题，深入研究菲律宾国家文化和艺术委员会（NCCA）如何制定政策和创造机制，以期为土著人民提供其文化传承所需的支持。自此这成为我持续的研究。过去十年里政策和机制是如何发展的？如今是否能对社区需求予以响应？

关键词：文化治理，文化政策，菲律宾

INTRODUCTION

A few months ago, I chanced upon the book on *Cultural Democracy: The Arts, Community, and the Public Purpose* by James Bau Graves, and was struck by the question he posed in his introduction: "What does your community need to keep its culture vital and meaningful?" This question made me reflect on my interest in intangible cultural heritage management and cultural policy, and the current conditions in the Philippines. In 2001, while I was still studying to be a dancer and thespian, I was intrigued by the cultures and artistic expressions of Indigenous people in the Philippines. I visited a couple of Indigenous communities in the Central and Southern Philippines. I watched their dances, listened to their songs, and noted their stories often asking questions on why and how they came about with what I just experienced. A few years following this immersion, I started on a research project on nurturing Indigenous culture and arts in the Philippines, taking a closer look at how the National Commission for Culture and the Arts (NCCA) in the Philippines formulated policies and created mechanisms to provide Indigenous people with the support they need to keep their cultures alive. This has been a constant inquiry of mine ever since. How have the policies and mechanisms developed in the past decade? Is it responsive to the needs of the communities?

MODELS OF CULTURAL POLICY, THE PHILIPPINE MODEL, AND THE ROLE OF THE NATIONAL COMMISSION FOR CULTURE AND THE ARTS (NCCA)

Governments traditional work with a "limited palette" when framing options or designing programs aimed at supporting arts and culture. Four historical models dominate the conversation on cultural policy, irrespective of the predisposition of the government (Craik 2007). These are the *facilitator*, the *patron*, the *architect*, and the *engineer* models. In the *facilitator* model, the government aims to create conditions that favor cultural production. In this model, cultural activities are subsidized by appropriating tax expenditures to provide tax relief or other benefits for those who give cultural support. In the *patron* model, the government directly supports the cultural and artistic forms that it favors. This model involves distributing funds directly, and largely through an "arm's length" mechanism. In the *architect* model, the government is directly involved in shaping the development of culture. This enables direct government funding, and relieves artists from dependence on "box office" mechanisms to survive. In the *engineer* model, the government owns the means of artistic production, and creators are employees whose creations are required to reflect the political agenda of the state in a positive light (Dingstad 2008).

Unlike other Southeast Asian countries where the Cultural Ministry holds sole authority in making decisions for cultural industries, the NCCA follows a hybrid policy model. Like most continental European countries, the NCCA acts as an *architect,* wherein it provides funding for culture and the arts and tends to support the arts as part of its social welfare objectives. It is through the NCCA that the government creates the framework for the country's cultural development, following the policy objectives and approaches stated in the Medium-Term Philippine Development Plan for Culture and the Arts (MTPDP-CA). In theory, the government makes final decisions about overall cultural policy regardless of the creation of public debates, conversations, consultations, or presentations to the NCCA.

Section five of Republic Act 7356 pushes for people to be actively involved within a climate of freedom and responsibility, in order to evolve and develop their culture and identity, thereby nurturing a Filipino national culture and identity. The NCCA operates from six guiding principles. First, the NCCA defines culture as a human right; thus, is a manifestation of the freedom of belief and expressions that need to be accorded due respect and be allowed to flourish. Second, the national identity of the Filipinos is reflected and shaped by their values, beliefs, and aspirations. Therefore, the Filipino national culture shall be evolved, promoted, and conserved. Third, culture is of the people, meaning that the Filipino national culture shall be independent, equitable, dynamic, progressive, and humanistic. Fourth, culture shall be evolved and developed by the people themselves within a climate of freedom and responsibility. Fifth, the creation of artistic and cultural products shall be promoted and disseminated to the greatest number of people, and shall be raised formally through the educational system and informally through extra-scholastic means, including the use of traditional and modern communications. Lastly, the NCCA must ensure that every citizen does their duty to preserve and conserve the Filipino historical and cultural heritage and resources.

Given this, the NCAA also follows an entity-relationship model, which is a common approach to "mapping" government cultural administrations, wherein entities such as agencies are actors in the cultural policy system and relationships are linkages between them. In effect, this makes the NCCA a *patron* for the arts. The NCCA determines the kind, type, and extent of support to individuals, groups, or communities and uses an arm's length mechanism to disburse funding support through national committees and sub-committees and their affiliated national cultural agencies. The NCCA works hand-in-hand with the Cultural Center of the Philippines, the Institute of Philippine Languages, the National Historical Institute, the National Library, the National Museum, and the Record Management and Archives Office.

The NCCA instituted four subcommissions working in different areas of the arts and culture sector. First is the Subcommission on the Arts (SCA), which has seven national committees representing each of the seven major art fields identified by the NCCA. The main objective of the SCA is to ensure standards of excellence in projects and activities supported by the NCCA. Through implementing policies, publishing funding information, and conducting workshops, seminars, and conferences where conversations happen on how best to achieve excellence and nurture Philippine art, the SCA can articulate its achievement of the core objective.

Second is the Subcommission on Cultural Dissemination (SCD), which is tasked with ensuring the widest dissemination of artistic and cultural works and products among the greatest number of people across the country and overseas for their appreciation and enjoyment (Flores 2010). It is important to highlight that the SCD is responsible for the establishment and development of culture and arts education programs at all levels of the educational system. It is equally important to note that culture and arts education programs can be done formally through the curriculum established by the Department of Education and informally through alternative settings, such as by having a cultural master to teach traditional skills or pass down intangible cultural heritage through the Schools of Living Traditions. Although the Schools of Living Traditions is a flagship initiative under the Subcommission on Cultural Communities and Traditional Arts (SCCTA), through informal or alternative dissemination of cultural information and education, the subcommissions collaborate or assist each other in the fulfillment of the mandate.

Third, the SCCTA is composed of three main cultural communities: The Northern cultural communities (Luzon islands), the Central cultural communities (Visayan islands), and the Southern cultural communities (island of Mindanao). The primary concern of the SCCTA is to address the needs of Indigenous communities all over the country, which is very challenging. Ma. Criselda Magsumbol (2010), the Culture and Arts Officer of the SCCTA, shares that the difficulty lies in the fact that most of these communities are scattered all over the archipelago, some communities belong to two groups, and several communities have been displaced because of natural and man-made calamities.

Fourth, the Subcommission on Cultural Heritage (SCH) is responsible for overseeing libraries and information services, archives, museums, galleries, monuments, and cultural sites. Together with the National Museum, the National Library, and the National Archives, the SCH conducts historical and scholarly research work, anthropological and archaeological studies, and produces publications to promote historical and cultural heritage.

Moreover, the NCCA continues to create local and provincial or regional councils as an additional structure in the implementation of national cultural policies. Rico Pableo Jr., the current Executive Director of the NCCA, shares that in order to further promote, develop, and protect the arts and culture in the Local Government Units, the Commission is working diligently to establish arts and cultural offices in municipalities (NCCA 2019).

In this hybrid model, one can see that there is an attempt to incorporate both "top-down" and "grassroots" approaches to cultural governance. Arguably, although final decisions on where and to whom funding and other support go lies ultimately with the NCCA, the platforms for public debates, conversations, consultations, and presentations to the NCCA and the recognition of various entities as active actors in the cultural policy system create a pluralistic approach to cultural governance; thus, there is a democratic approach because of the recognition of multiple publics. As pointed out in R.A. 7356, the national cultural law of the Philippines mandates equitable and pluralistic funding. Cultural policy, therefore, is designed to serve democratic objectives to guarantee artistic freedom by subsidizing the arts and to promote equal funding for all by funding centralized and decentralized cultural institutions.

I would like to point out that the NCCA did not explicitly articulate the fact that its framework is a hybrid of different public arts funding models. I superimposed different funding models on what I have observed being used by the NCCA for the purpose of discussion and in order to illustrate how this affects its policies and strategies for the funding of arts and culture. In fact, when I asked whether the NCCA had been consulted or was influenced by models of other countries, I received varying opinions. For instance, Corpuz (2010) mentioned that the NCCA consulted existing international conservation laws, such as UNESCO's and the Bura Charter of Japan. These laws were then adapted to the local setting of the communities in the Philippines. On the other hand, Dr. Peralta stressed that the NCCA framework was based on the context of the Philippines. The NCCA made sure that its approach is broad, flexible, and consultative because what will work for one community might not work for another. Thus, its system must be adaptable. Peralta (2010) said, "We know that our approach has to be specific in accordance with the parameters of society because if it is not, then society will reject it." Other staff members also believe that NCCA's model came out as a necessity of the communities, and that this is what they followed because there was no time or resources to consult other countries.

Table 1. Approved Budget Allocation for the SCA and SCCTA for 2007.

Subcommission	Amount in pesos	Amount in US dollars	Percentage allocation against overall budget
SCA	40 million	1.03 million	46%
SCCTA	6.7 million	173,000	12%

However, from 2005 to 2007, projects or initiatives under the SCA dwarfs the percentage share of funding given to the other subcommissions. In 2007 for example, SCA received a 46 percent share of the funding, which amounted to about 40 million pesos ($1.03 million USD). On the other hand, the percentage share of funding received by the SCCTA is only 12 percent or about 6.7 million pesos ($173,000 USD). From 2005 to 2007, there was a steady decline in percentage share of funding for SCCTA projects, from 19 percent in 2005 to 12 percent in 2007, while there was a slight increase in percentage share of funding for SCA projects, from 45 percent in 2005 to 46 percent in 2007 (NCCA 2010).

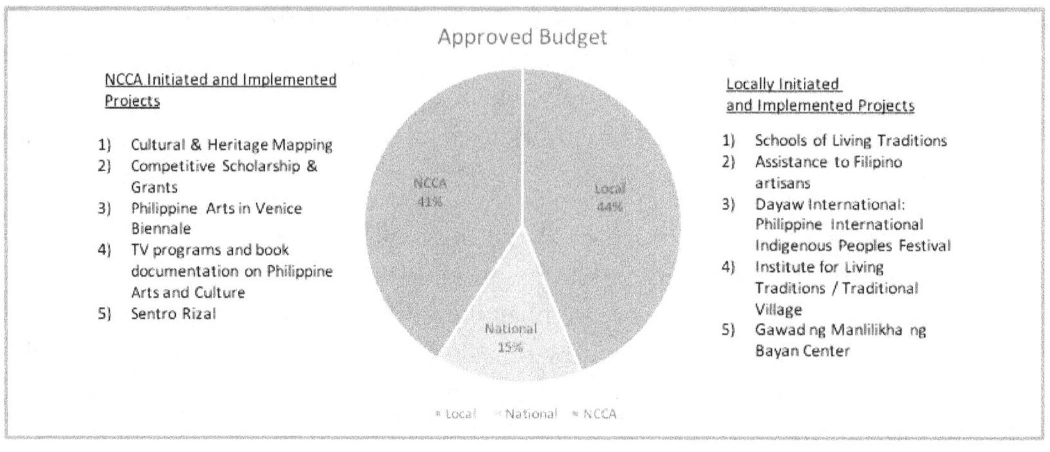

Figure 1. Locally-funded projects under the General Appropriations Act (as of December 2018).

By the end of December 2018, the NCCA disbursed a total of 188.45 million pesos (approximately $3.6 million USD) for funded projects under the General Appropriations Act (GAA) for that year. Fifty-six percent of this (106.2 million pesos or $2 million USD) went to projects under the national cultural agencies. Seventy-two percent of this 56 percent went to "direct" initiated projects of the NCCA. Foremost of these are *The Philippine Arts in Venice Biennale,* including participation in other contemporary art exhibitions, which had a budget of 45 million pesos; scholarships and grants, which were allocated 10 million pesos; and projects for cultural and heritage mapping and programs that disseminate cultural information and raise awareness within the greater public, such as the *Buhay na Buhay TV* program, the *2018 Sagisag Kultura TV* program, and a book on the *National Arts and Crafts Fair, which* received 15 million pesos (NCCA 2019).

On the other hand, 44 percent (82.25 million pesos or $1.6 million USD) of the total spending went to local cultural agencies, foundations, and organizations supporting projects such as alternative platforms for cultural preservation and dissemination to younger generations, efforts to safeguard intangible cultural heritage, assistance to Filipino artisans, creation of centers that support Indigenous artists, and scholarships and technical aid to train individuals for arts education in higher education (NCCA 2019).

Table B. Approved Budget Allocation for the SCA and SCCTA for 2018.

Subcommision	Amount in pesos	Amount in US dollars	Percentage allocation against overall budget
SCA	83 million	1.58 million	44%
SCCTA	74 million	1.40 million	39%

Comparing these numbers, more funding was arguably given to projects and initiatives under the SCA compared to projects and initiatives under SCCTA, at least for the years 2005-2007. The disparity in the percentage share of funding is evident and can be attributed to several factors. But quite positively, this disparity had been reduced significantly by the end of 2018. Breaking down the disbursed funding of 188.45 million pesos to the four subcommissions, one can see that approximately 83 million pesos went to SCA, 23 million pesos to SCD, 8 million pesos to SCH, and 74 million pesos to SCCTA. The increase in allocated funds for SCCTA projects and initiatives shows that more funds were disbursed outside of Metro Manila, and other big urban cities across the country. More funding has been shared to regional and rural areas and municipalities including ancestral sites of indigenous communities.

Unfortunately, a closer scrutiny shows that 59.5 percent of the total funding for local cultural agencies, foundations, and organizations went to the Non-Timber Forest Product-Exchange Program Incorporated Philippines (NTFP-EP), a collaborative network of non-government organizations (NGO) and community-based organizations (CBO) that acts as a mechanism that responds to the emerging needs of communities and assist organizations working on strengthening the capacity of forest-based communities towards a sustainable management of natural resources. Based on the 2018 Locally-Funded Projects Under the General Appropriations Act report, the NTFP-EP received a total of 49 million pesos of funding for initiatives such as *The Schools of Living Traditions* and the *Natural Indigo Dye* Centre, and projects to safeguard intangible cultural heritage and assist Filipino artisans.

This is not to devalue, belittle, or criticize the contribution of NTFP-EP to the development of rural and highly marginalized communities in the Philippines, nor to question its advocacy and efforts in the conservation and management of resources, and development of enterprises that has an obvious positive impact on the communities it serves. Instead, this is to highlight a potential problem in the mechanism and management of funding programs of the NCCA. Why does it seem that the allocation of support goes to a few? This question bellies the discourse on cultural governance and whether public funding for arts and culture is equally accessed and equitably distributed, arguing for the use of a more democratic means of cultural governance.

In the past decade, there have been several important developments in the cultural policy in the Philippines. In 2010, the NCCA finished implementing the Medium-Term Philippine Development Plan for Culture and the Arts (MTPDP-CA) for 2004 to 2010. MTPDP-CA was first shaped by the Philippine Development Plan for Culture and the Arts of 1999 to 2000. This was ratified during the administration of former President Fidel V. Ramos on April 7, 1993. This Plan focused on three programs: Institutional Building, Infrastructure Development, and Program Expansion. An important accomplishment of this Plan was the strengthening of the cultural network, and the building of cultural zones and offices, and the completion of the National Museum.

This Plan was continued in the Estrada Administration where continuous funding for culture and the arts was given by the state through the General Appropriations Act (GAA) and the National Endowment Fund for Culture and the Arts (NEFCA), a fund established exclusively for Philippine arts and culture programs, projects, and activities all over the country. It was also during the Estrada Administration that six other cultural agencies were attached to the NCCA for better policy and program coordination and collaboration through Executive Order 80.

In its second phase, the MTPDP-CA of 2004 to 2010 was approved by the Arroyo Administration. The rationale behind the MTPDP-CA was the recognition of the government of the potentials of culture as a catalyst for the promotion of peace and economic development. Its general strategy was the use of culture as a catalyst for values formation and human rights education, promoting a culture of peace, social justice, and sustainable development.

Two of the seven thrusts of MTPDP-CA were on these priorities: first, efforts directed to "mainstream culture and development in plans, policies, programs, and projects providing cultural services for the poor particularly the marginalized, the minorities and the migrants"; and second, the continued "implementation of programs for the promotions of cultural liberty and excellence in artistic development that forges the identity, memory, vision, and conscience of our nation" (MTPDP-CA 2011).

One of the most recent developments in the cultural policy of the Philippines is the proposed establishment of a Department of Culture sought by the NCCA and its partners in Congress in 2016. In 2017, the proposed establishment of a Department of Culture was filed as a priority bill, and was expected to be passed into law in 2019. With the Department of Culture is the creation of several bureaus: the Bureau of Cultural Communities and Traditional Arts Development, Bureau of Cultural Properties Protection and Regulation, Bureau of Cultural Properties Preservation, Bureau of Artistic Resources Development, Bureau of Cultural Research Education and Dissemination, and the Bureau of Cultural and Creative Industries.

How the creation of these bureaus will work towards a better policy and program coordination and collaboration remains to be seen in the next couple of years. Before investigating the outcomes of the new Department of Culture and the results and impact of the programs under each bureau, it is critical to look closely into the role of the NCCA this past decade. How, in its capacity, has it encouraged and allowed a democratic participation and governance of culture in the Philippines?

The NCCA has five major types of grants: competitive, institutional, outreach, Speakers Bureau Program, and grants that provide automatic financial assistance to affiliated agencies as governmental inter-agency support to promote synergy of efforts. These grants are dependent on the priority of the Office of the President—his/her vision and goals for the country's culture and the arts, in consultation with the Executive Director of the

NCCA. In spite of this dependence, the NCCA follows a core priority or direction that the President rarely changes. The core priorities or directions revolve around the seven needs defined in the MTPDPCA, namely: culture and development, culture and education, promotion of culture and arts, continued support for artistic excellence, conservation of cultural heritage; culture and peace, and culture and diplomacy.

The NCCA identifies the themes, objectives, design, and activities of the institutionalized programs. On the other hand, projects that are proposed to the NCCA for the competitive grants are designed by their proponents who are members of the communities or cultural sectors. Proposed projects must fall under the categories set by the NCCA to ensure that they are anchored on the set goals; and follows bureaucratic rules, regulations, and procedures. Despite this, Savior (2010), a member of NCCA's National Committee on Dramatic Arts, explains, "The goals or themes of the NCCA are only a backbone. It can be interpreted in different ways. The theme can be fundamentally followed. But it can also be metaphorically linked or interpreted to a specific localization of a specific need of the committee. So it is the committee that will decide what its policy will be at a given time."

This duality can be very confusing, which can lead to various problems and misinterpretations or misrepresentation. Although ideas from the national agency and from the grassroots level eventually meet in the middle, and mediated by the National Advisory Board (NAB), there still lies the concern about whether what is presented at the discussion table truly represents the needs and concerns of the communities. Savior (2010) shared, "In some of our meetings, we lobby our needs. That is why we can form our programs. But this is tricky because the committee in Manila will push for something which for us in Mindanao is not favorable, or it will put the communities in Mindanao at a disadvantage."

Another point of concern is precisely this. The committee in Manila or the National Capital Region, which historically has clout on what gets approved or considered, might treat other regions or clusters parochially. The beauty of the NCCA's framework is that this concern gets to be checked to prevent having an *imperialistic* Manila. The NCCA's framework is designed to have equal representation from the National Committees on Northern, Central, and Southern Cultural Communities. But the problem is on who sits in the National Advisory Board (NAB), who ultimately decides on this matter? Are votes on the NAB equally distributed among regions? According to the Implementing Rules and Regulations of the NCCA, the NAB is composed of the heads of the National Committees under the four Subcommissions. Here lies the problem because there is inequity in the number of representatives, which means inequity in the number of votes. The SCH has six national committees, entitling it to six votes. The SCD and SCCTA only have three national committees, thus they only have three votes. But the SCA has seven national committees, thus it has seven votes, which means more voting power. These numbers show us that votes are not equally distributed among regions or specialized areas. In effect, cultural policies that are threshed out by the National Advisory Board leans more towards policies for contemporary arts. Despite their majority number, Savior (2010) shares that a problem still exists on whether the voices of the representatives from the south are accommodated by the traditionally dominant group that comes from the National Capital Region.

Understanding cultural governance and the Philippine situation

The Philippine society is culturally strongly Euro-American having been under Spanish and American rule for almost four centuries. But at the same time, it is culturally diverse with more than a hundred ethnolinguistic groups. The indigenous peoples in the Philippines have a very rich and diverse culture and cultural expressions from the *Bontoc, Ifugaos,* and *Kalinga's* in Northern Luzon to groups in the Visayas who have assimilated and acculturated to Christian Filipinos to the *Katawhang Lumads* in the highlands of Mindanao.

In understanding cultural governance in the Philippine context, one has to acknowledge the prevailing debate between being 'Manila-centric' versus a push for regional cultural governance and administration of public support for the arts. The geographic, the Philippines is an archipelago with 7,641 islands, and cultural, has 182 living languages divided into 17 regions—16 of which are Administrative Divisions and 1 Autonomous Region in Muslim Mindanao (ARMM), make-up of the Philippines heavily shape and influence the said debate.

To understand cultural governance, one has to consider that the term itself is challenging to define or elucidate because of the complexity of what is being governed, culture. Culture is highly abstract, and its governance through certain policies does not take into account its nature. More often than not, the conversation on cultural policy and governance happens within closed doors among experts, and platforms for public dialogues and debates are mere tokens of a democratic process. The Philippines' concept of democracy is borrowed from American democracy—the ideology "of the people, by the people, for the people." But is democracy in the Philippines truly democratic, wherein the voices of many and the sentiments of the 'publics' are heard? To be democratic means to be fair, equitable, proportional, and transparent in the representation of all in the process of building a civic society. Graves (2005) warns us that, as coined from historian and educator Benjamin Barber, empowering the merely ignorant and endow the uneducated with a right to make collective decisions and what results is not democracy but, at best, mob rule. Democracy is a sham unless everyone has an equal opportunity to be heard, and the contributions of many are needed to find democratic solutions. Cultural democracy offers a different paradigm, a system of support for the cultures of our diverse communities that are respectful and celebratory, that gives voice to the many who have been historically excluded from the public domain, and that makes no claims of superiority or special status (Graves 2005).

What has the NCCA done in this regard? In its work on cultural governance, has it created a system or mechanism that truly supports the arts and cultural projects of the various communities in the Philippines, regardless of language and location or proximity to central Manila?

The answer to this may be a resounding 'yes'. Constitutionally through Republic Act 7356, the NCCA is bound to uphold the following governing principles: culture as human rights, national identity, culture of the people, culture by the people, culture for the people, and preservation of Filipino heritage. It is important to highlight that the NCCA was created to safeguard the culture of the people. Section four of R.A.7356 states that the Filipino national culture shall be independent, equitable, dynamic, progressive, and humanistic (NCCA 1994). Culture, being independent, should be free of any political and economic structures, which inhibit cultural sovereignty. Equitability is defined as providing opportunities to the poor and marginalized sectors. The Filipino national culture, defined to be dynamic, means that it must continuously develop in pace with scientific, technological, social, economic, and political changes both on national and international levels. Therefore, the NCCA must create avenues or means for these sectors to grow, and for their culture to develop amidst the social and economic changes. Moreover, it must ensure the creative and artistic freedom of every Filipino to achieve his or her potential.

Section five of this Act expresses that the Filipino national culture shall evolve and be developed by the people themselves in a climate of freedom and responsibility (NCCA 1994). Therefore, the national cultural policies and programs must be for the benefit of all. The Philippines is a country of diverse culture, having mentioned earlier that it has over a hundred ethnolinguistic communities. Therefore, the NCCA must acknowledge and respect the diversity of cultural identities, and needs to adopt or use a pluralistic approach to respond to the said diversity of culture. Furthermore, national cultural policies and programs must also be democratic and non-partisan. Bernan Joseph Corpuz (2010), the Head of the Planning and Policy Office of the NCCA, states, "We have to cater to all. We cannot favor contemporary and modern art and artists or only indigenous communities." He further asserts that "[It] is a conscious effort in the sense that as much as possible we [NCCA] want to give equal funding to all aspects of culture and the arts." Thus, reinforcing that the policy of the NCCA encourages and supports the individual or group, regardless of creed, affiliation, ideology, ethnic origin, age, gender, or class—including the marginalized sectors. State support cannot be monopolized by any group or sector.

For the NCCA to achieve what it is mandated to do, it created a Secretariat to do the administrative and legal work of extending and disbursing financial and technical support to arts and cultural organizations, institutions, and communities. As discussed previously, the NCCA created the four subcommissions and the national committees to aid the national office and fulfill its pluralistic mandate. The pluralistic approach is further manifested in how the NCCA encourages and facilitates the organization of a network of regional and local councils for culture and the arts. This is to ensure a broad nationwide, people-based participation in the formulation of plans, implementation of projects and programs, and the review of funding requirements.

Advocating for the NCCA, one can argue that it fulfills its mandate through addressing the needs of various communities, and providing them access to the 'round table' where their sentiments and views are heard and considered. One only needs to use the main programs of the NCCA, coupled with it being an *architect* and *patron* in its arts funding model, to provide evidence to support such an argument. The NCCA Grants Program has five major types all responding to the different needs of the culture and arts sector. First, the Competitive Grant has the widest appeal because it caters to individual or group projects specific to the focus of each national committee. Applications or proposals usually come from urban or regional artists who have convenient access to information from the NCCA. Second, the Institutional Grants provide financial resources for institutionalized programs such as the Philippine International Arts Festival, Filipino Heritage Month, National Artists Award, and the *Gawad sa Manlilikha ng Bayan* (National Living Treasures) Award. Third, there are also grants for outreach programs, which are geared towards providing projects for marginalized communities. Lastly, are the grants for the Speakers Bureau Program, which provides professionals fees and travel funds for experts who then give capacity building trainings and workshops to communities across the country. This is to ensure that everyone will have the adequate training to be able to navigate through the grant schemes of the NCCA and the bureaucratic process, but more importantly, to be able to effectively and/or efficiently manage arts and cultural projects.

Furthermore, the NCCA has established the Philippine Cultural Education Program (PCEP) in 17 project sites in 2002. The PCEP is a comprehensive five-year medium term plan from 2003 to 2007 formed by government and non-government organization that lay out the goals, policies, programs, and projects on cultural education through the formal, non-formal, and informal education systems. The use of both the English and Filipino languages creates a unique impact on the education system in the Philippines. Although based on the American system where English is the medium of instruction, Philippine schools put equal emphasis on academics and social and cultural aspects. Culture thus becomes the foundation of education, sustainable development, and governance because of the adoption of a culture-based education. Through a culture-based education, the NCCA and the Department of Education created an educational system that nurtures a sense of belonging and identity, and strengthens community participation; as well as promotes appreciation and understanding of one's history and cultural heritage. Moreover, through the PCEP, the NCCA offers the Certificate Program in Culture-Based Governance to local government units. That is why there are still on-going projects on cultural and heritage mapping that the NCCA continues to fund and support. The NCCA recognizes the crucial role of the communities' culture in teaching and learning. In the province of Batangas for example, Batangueno music, literature, traditions, dance, food, and the arts are used to reinforce the learning of students and make them reflect on the characteristics of a way or approach in life that is distinctively Batangueno. Thus, culture-based education is used to instill a sense of national pride and develop an individual's identity as a nation. But more importantly, by preserving the cultural memory, it is hoped that an individual will have a greater understanding of the nation's destiny amongst a community of nations. In general, "culture shall be utilized as a catalyst for values formation and human rights education, promoting a culture of peace, social justice, and sustainable development" (MTPDP-CA 2007-2010).

However, the resounding 'yes' that the NCCA has created a system or a mechanism that truly supports the arts and cultural projects of communities all over the Philippines is not devoid of problems or gaps. The organization of regional and local arts and cultural councils and the creation of the PCEP has indeed helped in the dissemination of information about the funding and technical support that the NCCA and its affiliates provide to various communities. But the inherent geographical make-up of the Philippines still posts a major problem in the dissemination of information, and therefore, it creates problems in the dissemination of support. This is especially true to indigenous cultural communities in far-flung areas where access to transportation and communication is extremely difficult.

The NCCA also lacks the needed manpower to reach far-flung communities. Thus, the NCCA relies heavily on the national committee members or community representatives to assist them in information dissemination. Magsumbol (2010) shared that, "The committee members are our contact to the communities. We depend on them because some communities are so far that we can no longer go to them." She also shared that communicating and coordinating with community representatives is also difficult as these representatives may not have easy access to communication tools, or it takes them days to travel from their communities to the town proper where access to telephones and the internet are available.

To solve this problem, the communities elect representatives who live closer to town centers and have better access to communication. The problem with this is that it goes against the idea of decentralization. Because the NCCA does not have satellite offices, it needs to have as many contacts from different regions, municipalities, and towns. What is ideal is that these contacts come from the communities both near or far from town centers as much as possible. But this is not the case. The reality is that community representatives live in town centers and no longer with their communities, to have access to communication; thus, somewhat undermining the mandate of the Subcommission, especially that of the SCCTA, to promote and disseminate the creation of artistic and cultural products to the greatest number of Filipino people.

Adding to this problem is the fact that most SCCTA staff and community representatives are not adequately trained as anthropologists or cultural administrators. Peralta (2010) explains, "A lot of people in the NCCA are not trained as anthropologists or sociologists, as well as the community representatives that are consulted. People who are elected are political figures whose backgrounds are not on culture but other areas. They propose a project for ethnic groups without understanding the purpose of the project for the ethnic group." Thus, there is a need to review the system and mechanism in place to have the ideas, opinions, and insights from the communities reconciled and validated. Despite its limitations, the NCCA needs to find a way to expand the Speakers Bureau Program to provide the information and technical assistance needed by the communities and their representatives.

Issues in cultural governance in the Philippines

In spite of the formulated policies, and the initiatives, programs, and development work done by the NCCA towards the arts and culture in the Philippines, it still faces several issues foremost is on transparency and diversification, and patronage and conflict of interests. In terms of its organization, is the NCCA's governance through committees and cluster representatives, whether appointed or elected, ensure a democratic process? In terms of the process of governance, how exactly are the members of the committees chosen? Who exactly is marginalized by these choices?

Madden (2009) argues that effective civil society participation in the governance of culture is achieved not by the set-up of additional institutions, but by the degree of independence from the government. Unfortunately, as argued by Holden (2006), the problem with cultural governance is that cultural policy is a closed conversation among experts rather than a democratic mandate from the public; and this reality seems to be true in the Philippines. Corpuz (2010) explains the alignment of visions of the government and the cultural communities, that both visions are 'married and weaved' through the NCCA's model as an architect and patron. Corpuz (2010) shares that, fortunately, what the culture and arts sector identifies as its vision aligns with the government's goals specifically on the development of the Filipino national culture and identity. Mark Dela Cruz (2016), from the Program Monitoring and Evaluation Division of the NCCA, states that the committees and cluster representatives hold the responsibility as well as the power to voice the issues of their respective communities, bring them to the attention of the NCCA and propose resolutions together with their fellow representatives.

But there is a problem here. If the culture and arts sector often, if not always, identifies as projects, resolutions, or initiatives align with the government's goal, it brings into question if the communities through the representatives are merely playing the funding game and are reshaping the needs and voices of the communities they represent accordingly. The reality of this alignment to gain public funding and support also discounts the fundamental acceptance of differences. Rather than assisting the communities, collectives, and individuals in their cultural development in multiple directions, such process reinforces a top-down approach where the dominant culture still comes from the elite institutions, or in this case from the director and heads of the Commission. When asked how the National Endowment Fund for Culture and the Arts is allocated, Corpuz (2010) shares, "Most of the budget, at least 50% is allocated to the competitive grants and opened to grassroots projects. This is to give communities a bigger chance to submit and get funding from the programs set by the four subcommissions, so we align the vision of the culture and arts sector to the vision of the government. Because if the vision of the culture and arts sector is not aligned to the government, then no funding will be given." Cultural professionals have focused on satisfying the policy demands of their funders in an attempt to gain the same unquestioning support for culture, that exists for health or education, but the truth is that politicians will never be able to give that support until there exists a more broadly based and better articulated democratic consensus (Holden 2006), and this highlights the situation between the relationship of the NCCA and the arts and cultural sector. However, when it comes to traditional arts, Peralta (2010) insists that the NCCA does not intervene in the decisions of the indigenous communities. According to Peralta, no matter what the NCCA does to preserve a certain cultural product, whether it is tangible or intangible if the community will not exert the effort, the initiative will fail. The NCCA does encourage and influence the community to make the proper decisions.

Santiago (2016) alluded to the issue, where she argued that government appointments need to be questioned and scrutinized because relationships brought about by said appointments to positions are primarily based on the *Padrino* system, which is a "mentorship" system that is about who you know, not what your skills are—and tends to keep the opportunities within the very small circle that the cultural establishment sustains. Santiago, perhaps, was talking about the controversial appointment of Freddie Aguilar, a veteran singer-songwriter but has not headed any cultural organizations or has been a commissioner of the NCCA, to be the Head of the NCCA. Aguilar was called by the president's executive assistant on the possibility of heading the NCCA. Before this, Aguilar, who is a staunch supporter of Duterte who is the current president of the Philippines, asked Duterte to create a department for culture and the arts where he plans to lead a cultural revolution. The obvious problem with this is that it is not within the President's authority to appoint the head of the NCCA. Section 9 of the Republic Act 7356 states that the chairperson of the commission is elected by a 15-member Board of Commissioners. It is exactly these closed-door decisions and disregard of established processes that highlight the *Padrino* system. One can argue that the problem of cultural governance in the Philippines is that it is a dysfunctional or false democracy. It is, in reality, a feudal system of governance specifically pointing towards the relationship between the lord and vassal, where the lord and vassal have agreed on obligations to one another. Such a relationship creates a very small counsel of people in power where decisions are made based on their views. How then is the voice of the people being heard?

The *Padrino* system may already be very well present in the NCCA. Looking at the current structure and organization of the NCCA, one can see that most of the members of the Commission are appointed to their positions, and those who occupy these positions may not necessarily come from the culture and arts sector or have substantial knowledge and understanding of what is happening in the sector. Amongst the members of the Commission, only four come from the private sector, where three are the elected heads of the Subcommissions on Cultural Heritage, Arts, and Cultural Dissemination. Appointments to political or cultural positions that make decisions for the society may not necessarily be a problem as long as such appointments observe agreed upon democratic processes. Moreover, information on such process is readily available to the public, and that those who are appointed or elected within the commission, represent the very communities they serve. Failure to do so results in the issue of *delicadeza*, a behavior anchored on general accepted moral standards because it questions who the committees and cluster representatives truly represent.

To address this concern, Arlene Flores, a project development officer of the NCCA, argues otherwise. Flores (2010) explains that the NCCA's process is unique and organic to the agency. It is very democratic, at least in Asia, in its approach because of the structure of the Subcommissions and national committees that consist of more than a hundred experts in various fields; and are reflective of the Filipino culture. Flores further explains that these experts who are volunteer members of the national committees are consulted regularly. Ninety percent of the members of the national committees come from the private sector. This demographic is highly valued by the NCCA because these national committee members voice the needs and concerns of the communities since they are directly in communication with them. Without the involvement of the private sector, it will be highly improbable that the NCCA would know and understand the needs of the different cultural sectors.

To be democratic is to ensure that the wealth of cultures is practiced openly, and not behind closed doors, or else it will diminish. To be democratic demands a more accurate work in providing an equitable spotlight on moments and needs that call for a response, and that the communities themselves are seated in the decision-making table. Perhaps there is a better way and a more honest representation across the culture and arts sector, which, as Santiago (2016) proposes, entails a review on the right to vote within the sectors regardless if the individual is or is not part of any structured organization, or is not well connected within the network of artists, practitioners, or administrators. It also entails a review of representation across generations of artists and scholars, demanding for more diversity. Doing so enables people to participate in policy decisions that affect the quality of their cultural lives, assuring fair and equitable access to cultural resources and support. Moreover, it saves the NCCA from falling into the trap of patronage of keeping the same circle of people in positions of power. When we take into consideration the cultural institutions' loss of authority, the cultural liberation, we might expect a cultural policy turn that points toward the contribution to negotiations on meaning, with value in our everyday life as an independent purpose (Juncker & Balling 2016). With this in mind, it might be necessary for the NCCA to review, if in its process of institutionalizing a lot of its programs and initiatives, has it empowered the communities and arts sector to speak, participate and contribute.

Thus, it is extremely important to know who are the actors in cultural governance in the Philippines. What are their motivations, and where does the power reside? With over a hundred ethnolinguistic communities, cultural governance in the country is faced with webs of ethnicity and affiliations, political or otherwise, that need to be navigated. Although certain levels of trust are given to the committee members and cluster representatives, it can also be argued that communities are likely to view the ideas, statements, and actions of these committee members and representatives with varying degrees of suspicion. Underlying here is the fact that committee members and cluster representatives, although having institutional authority, cannot be fully informed or effective, which then reinforces that artists, cultural practitioners, and members of the communities are at the bottom of the hierarchy. How can they be lifted to be part of the table where important discussions on the governance of culture take place?

Gattinger (2011) opens three main ideas for debate and discussion on these perspectives. First, the democratization of culture and cultural democracy can be most effectively pursued by public arts funders if they do so through the lens of governance and multi-level governance. In this context, governance means encompassing, non-hierarchical, decentralized, and collaborative policy-making approaches between interdependent public, private, and civic actors (2011: 4). Second, public arts funders should carefully analyze the possible repercussions for the democratization of culture and culture democracy of making fundamental changes to existing governance arrangements between business, government, and society (Gattinger 2011: 4). Third, public arts funders would do well to identify the multi-level governance arrangements best suited to pursuing the democratization of culture and cultural democracy. This involves identifying the most supportive coordination arrangements for the democratization of culture and cultural democracy and identifying which aspects of democratization of culture and cultural democracy should be pursued by which level of government (Gattinger 2011: 5).

In this conversation of multi-level governance in the Philippines, Gattinger's arguments demand us to look microscopically on the arts administrator or cultural mediator who is at the crux between the government and national cultural institutions and the communities across regions and provinces in the country. As Graves (2005) stresses, the arts administrator or cultural mediator holds a significant power within its spheres of influence, and this highlights how far down the economic food chain artists and communities are. The mediator mediates several distinct realms between the artists, communities, funding sources, and the red tape of civic bureaucracy. This also makes cultural mediators the glue that holds things in place for something to happen. The mediator is in this powerful and influential, but very important position, as this power and influence, demands him to navigate and manage the enormous knowledge and commitment of the other actors in cultural governance both from the government and the communities.

Graves (2005) further shares that it is important to understand that the cultural mediator cannot make anything happen without the community, but often the community cannot budge without the facilitation of the mediator. But what seems to be ironic is that for a cultural mediator to be successful, he has to be willing to give the power away to others at every turn (Graves 2005). This brings us back to the argument earlier that governance is non-hierarchical, and instead encompassing and decentralized, where policy-making takes on collaborative approaches. This is not to argue that the NCCA changes its structure and model of arts funding. Instead, it encourages and suggests to the NCCA the imperative need to review, how in its hybrid model of reconciling the vision, views, and voices of the national agency and the communities in the grassroots level are considered in the shaping of cultural policy, and the creation or development of mechanisms that will create far more effective dissemination of financial and technical support to cultural communities across the country; and through this redefine the role of the NAB, and address the issues of transparency and diversification, and patronage. As argued by Juncker and Balling (2016), we need to consider a culture that takes place outside institutions, and without gatekeepers and mediators, and develop cultural policies and arts advocacies that allow interconnected and peer-driven interaction and collaboration.

This then pushes the NCCA to engage in more long-term collaborations with local government units, cultural agencies and institutions, the Department of Education, non-government organizations, the private sector, and most importantly, the arts and cultural communities. The NCCA has to understand that to pursue a more democratic cultural governance, it has to realize that the concept of community itself is as varied as the perspectives of its members. Therefore, the NCCA has to facilitate and help the community members find agreement on a clear sense of itself as a coherent group, and not define the said identity for the community through representation. This is for the committee and cluster representatives to understand, that the sector or the community they represent do not have a singular voice; that each community functions differently with their own set of priorities or values most important to them; and that every community is diverse, and who gets to be invited in policy conversations and planning for the community needs to be thought through to not inadvertently alienate a whole segment of the community. Also, one has to understand that community culture is personal wherein the appointed or elected 'leaders' may not necessarily be the pillars, movers, or shakers of the community. Therefore, the said leaders must not make decisions on behalf of any community. In a democracy, participation is key; thus, no individual should be in a position to dictate the content or method of others' cultural consumption, or the public representation of others' cultures. Lastly, democratic cultural governance considers that the artists or cultural practitioners, communities, and institutions all need each other—that in the dialogic process, all three must be able to convey adequately their aspirations, values, and needs to others. To enable progress and move in the right direction, these three actors must understand each others' value positions clearly, and recognize their respective legitimacy and limitations.

CONCLUSION

Johann Wolfgang von Goethe once said, "Which is the best government? That which teaches us to govern ourselves."

This paper has shown that with its hybrid funding model and governing principles, the NCCA has successfully established a structure, formulated policies, created mechanisms, and nurtured linkages with affiliate government agencies and cultural institutions, regional councils, and local government units in the governance of culture in the Philippines. Despite the limitations in resources and challenges faced in enacting its mandate, given the geographical make-up of the country and the hundreds of communities it has to serve, the NCCA continues to respond equitably and fairly to the various arts and cultural sectors, and in the process, has achieved its mandate.

However, the NCCA needs to realize that to answer the question on whose to govern for whose good, it needs to look toward the people who are closest to the issues of the cultural communities because they deal directly with the dynamic relationships and changes on the ground. This asks the NCCA to reimagine the cultural governance of communities as a regional governance process where the said process uses the communities' traditional rules, values, and systems of social organization to reimagine their contemporary governance needs and solutions. This then leads to the consideration of nodal networks as a model of a pluralistic approach to cultural governance. A nodal network is formed by the interconnectedness and interdependence of essentially autonomous units and actors, where the constituent linkages can facilitate or inhibit the functioning of the overall system. New governance institutions should be initiated by the people themselves, based on their informed consent.

In this light, the NCCA needs to look into existing collectives and networks of artists, cultural practitioners, and leaders to study and understand how they bring community members together to undertake programs, activities, and initiatives that resonate with community members' views; thus, what is considered is culturally legitimate and workable for the community. By empowering community members, the NCCA is able to create a culture of accountability and responsibility, which is a valuable asset in governance. An empowered community, one where the voices and sentiments of the community are heard and sets a consensus agenda among its members, and not simply wait for directions or directives from a national office, makes community participation or involvement simple, enjoyable, and meaningful for a member. This is not to argue that the concept of selecting a few to govern the many is ineffective and breeds incompetence. Instead, it is to embrace a pluralistic mindset to governance.

This also brings the conversation to a greater focus on important elements that can build a smooth, efficient, and effective governance structure specific to the context and realities of a community. It goes beyond cultural governance as an academic topic. Instead, it is a conversation that works toward structures, mechanisms, processes, and approaches that are sensitive and able to be shaped by public opinion. The conversation then turns from the centralization versus decentralization argument to a conversation on désétatisation, or the removal of state control, to allow shifts in governance within regions and within the synergy of the public, private, non-profit and civic actors. Therefore, cultural governance becomes a combination of horizontal, vertical, and lateral collaborations. It becomes a value-based governance, rather than a hierarchy-based relationship.

REFERENCES

Corpuz, Bernan Joseph. (2010) Interviewed by author, August 31.

Craik, Jennifer. (2007) *Re-Visioning Arts and Cultural Policy*. Australia: Australia National University Press.

Dela Cruz, Mark. (2016) Interviewed by author, April 29.

Dingstad, Christopher. (2008) The Increasing Importance of Private Arts Funding in Norway. *Master's thesis, Teachers College, Columbia University.*

Flores, Arlene. (2010) Interviewed by author, August 23.

Gattinger, M. (2011) Democratization of Culture, Cultural Democracy and Governance. Paper presented at the Canadian Public Arts Funders Annual General Meeting, Whitehorse, Yukon, November 16-18.

Graves, James Brau. (2005) *Cultural Democracy: The Arts, Community, and the Public Purpose*. Chicago, IL: University of Illinois Press.

Holden, John. (2006) Cultural Policy is a Closed Conversation Among Experts. What Culture Needs is a Democratic Mandate From The Public ... In *Cultural Value and the Crisis of Legitimacy: Why Culture Needs a Democratic Mandate*. London, UK: Demos.

Juncker, B., and G. Balling. (2016) The Value of Art and Culture in Everyday Life: Towards an Expressive Cultural Democracy. *The Journal of Arts Management, Law, and Society*, 46 (5): 231–242.

Madden, Christopher. (2009) The Independence of Government Arts Funding: A Review. *D'Art Topics in Arts Policy* 9: 16. Sydney, Australia: International Federation of Arts Councils and Culture Agencies.

Magsumbol, Ma. Criselda. (2010) Interviewed by author, August 24.

National Commission for Culture and the Arts. (1994) Republic Act No. 7356. Intramuros, Manila: National Commission for Culture and the Arts.

National Commission for Culture and the Arts. (2010) NCCA Term Report 2005–2007: Three Years of Culture and Arts for National Identity and Sustainable Development. Intramuros, Manila: National Commission for Culture and the Arts.

National Commission for Culture and the Arts. (2011) Medium Term Philippine Development Plan for Culture and the Arts. *National Commission for Culture and the Arts.* <http://www.ncca.gov.ph/about-ncca/programs/mtpdp/about-ncca-chapter 01.php> (Accessed 14 January 2011).

National Commission for Culture and the Arts. (2019) Locally Funded Projects under the General Appropriations Act as of Dec. 2018. *National Commission for Culture and the Arts.* <https://ncca.gov.ph/wp-content/uploads/2019/01/Status-2018-GAA-Fund-101-Locally-Funded-Projects-LFP.xls> (Accessed 22 May 2019).

National Commission for Culture and the Arts. (2019) NCCA Secretariat <https://ncca.gov.ph/about-ncca-3/the-secretariat.php> (Accessed 1 October 2019).

Peralta, Jesus. (2010) Interviewed by author, September 7.

Santiago, Katrina Stuart. (2016) The Situation of Arts and Culture. *The Manila Times.* <https://manilatimes.net/2016/08/20/opinion/columnists/the-situation-of-arts-and-culture/281039/> (Accessed 11 January 2019).

Savior, Hobart. (2010) Interviewed by author, September 5.

PLAY AS A FOUNDATION OF COMMON GOOD

ALEX TAM

Centre for Research and Development in Visual Arts,
Hong Kong Baptist University

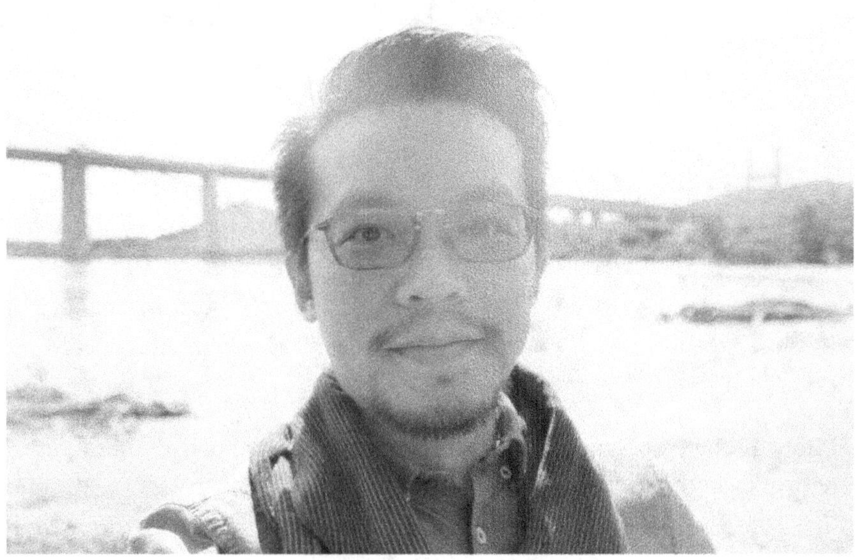

Alex Tam is a Clore Fellow of 2015 who is experienced in working on art projects that engage with issues connected to the notion of history, memory, collective learning and place-making. He is the Centre Executive of the Centre for Research and Development in Visual Arts, Hong Kong Baptist University, which plays an important role in the cultural landscape in Hong Kong for knowledge exchange, as well as being a community hub for the visual culture in Hong Kong. In 2016, he co-founded Play Depot, an open-for-all community playground based in To Kwa Wan, a used-to-be industrial district, in Hong Kong, that encourages social interaction and creative play among local residents; enhance social engagement among themselves and with the public realm at large.

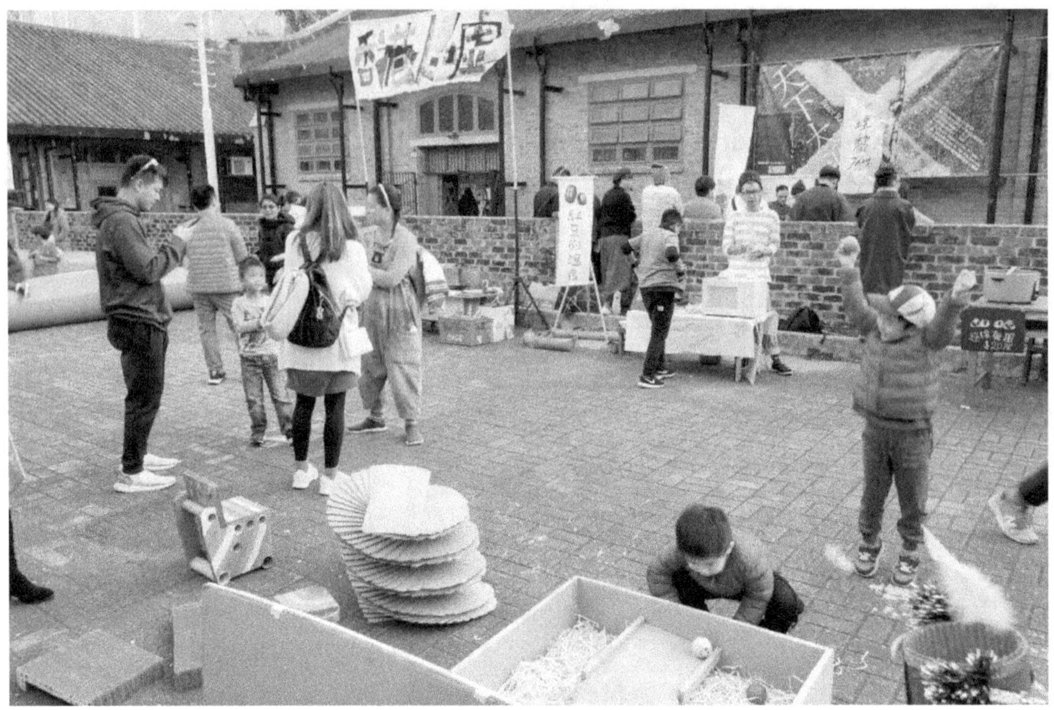

Photo 1. The Play Depot connects residents with a supportive community network where various activities are self-organised.

Hong Kong has faced escalating social turmoil and growing hatred towards the government, especially the police force, for abuse of power since June 2019 (Yu and Kuo 2019). Public anger is on-going due to the government's failure to lead honestly and listen deeply to public concerns (Cheng 2019). Evidence of police brutality and collusion has been circulating in many media reports, both local and international (Amnesty International Hong Kong 2019; Chan 2019; Hernández et al. 2019; Mahtani et al. 2019). This is not merely a political issue, but an ethical flaw that has tremendous social consequences and has reached the critical point of destroying people's lives and wellness and the social contract. At a time of tremendous divisiveness in society, I have seen friends and families break apart due to different political views, neighbours lose trust in others, and people suffer from mental breakdown and give up their life (Haas 2019; Lai 2019; Time 2019). As an art practitioner working to foster civic awareness and achieve an egalitarian, inclusive, fair, and just society through public practice, I felt disgruntled and resentful towards the Hong Kong government for their inability to uphold universal values and morals. The current conflict affects my work considerably. I am unwilling to be dragged into this awful situation, but no one can be shielded from the negative impact that the current crisis has upon us. It has left me no choice but to postpone or even cancel most planned public activities for the past three months, partly as a precautionary measure to reduce the safety risk for visitors and partly as a way of sending an urgent message to authorities and the outside world that our city is entering into an unprecedented crisis in which the old norms no longer exist and widespread deception is the new norm. In many ways, it has been a dark time, but I realised that despite the endless hurt that people in Hong Kong are experiencing, a healing process could happen at the same time to develop resilience in the face of difficulties and crises. Since October 2019, our project has slowly been picking up the momentum and resuming again.

In fact, this terrible situation is not unfamiliar to me. I can still remember the disappointment and frustration people had five years ago as many consider the Umbrella Movement—a pro-democracy political movement in 2014 that resulted in a seventy-nine-day occupation of the city centre demanding universal suffrage for the 2017 chief executive election (BBC 2019)—to be a complete failure. This generated increasingly widespread apathy and anxiety among students, young people, artists, and society at large towards social and political issues.

This article, written on the occasion of the fifth anniversary of the Umbrella Movement in Hong Kong, describes the sentiment and state of mind in which I co-founded Play Depot with my artist friends three years ago. Our first impulse in responding to the situation was to use artistic means to produce counter-narratives. We reckoned that it is essential to create a "safe" space that allows us to cope with our vulnerabilities, uncertainties, ambiguities, and strengths.

Located in a century-old animal quarantine depot (a Grade II listed heritage building now transformed into an artist village) in a former industrial district in Hong Kong, Play Depot is a socially engaged art project that aims to promote a sense of place in residents and incite people's creativity and imagination through creative play. Our long-term ambition is to shift public participation in art and culture away from indifference, passive consuming to active participating and producing. We believe that two key elements can make this transformation possible: creativity and playfulness. A specific question that guides our work therefore is this: how can play be used to create spaces that promote creative thinking and action, communication, interaction, and trust?

As an open-for-all community playground, it was founded upon ideals that encourage social interaction and creative play among local residents, and enhance social engagement among themselves and with the public at large. We embrace openness and generosity, which underpin the values of the project. We explore playful ways that help us step out into uncharted terrain with a long-term view to mediate difference in an increasingly fragmented community.

The site is an open playground that provides playful and creative workshops and activities. The project is popular among children and their parents from different social hierarchies, who play and participate in games with each other (Photo 1).

The neighbouring area of our space faces impeding gentrification and a lack of public space for either adults or children, due to business-driven urban redevelopment. Many new immigrants from mainland China and South Asian countries, such as Nepal, Pakistan, and India, have settled in the area because of the relatively affordable rental rates. Most of them are low-income workers with unstable working status. However, as many new high-rise residential and commercial buildings have displaced the old ones where people used to live, the social fabric of the neighbourhood is changed rapidly by gentrification. Apart from that, lots of parks and playgrounds in the area have been turned into construction sites for the MTR in To Kwa Wan. The lack of playground area and family-friendly facilities is a big concern for the community (Photo 2).

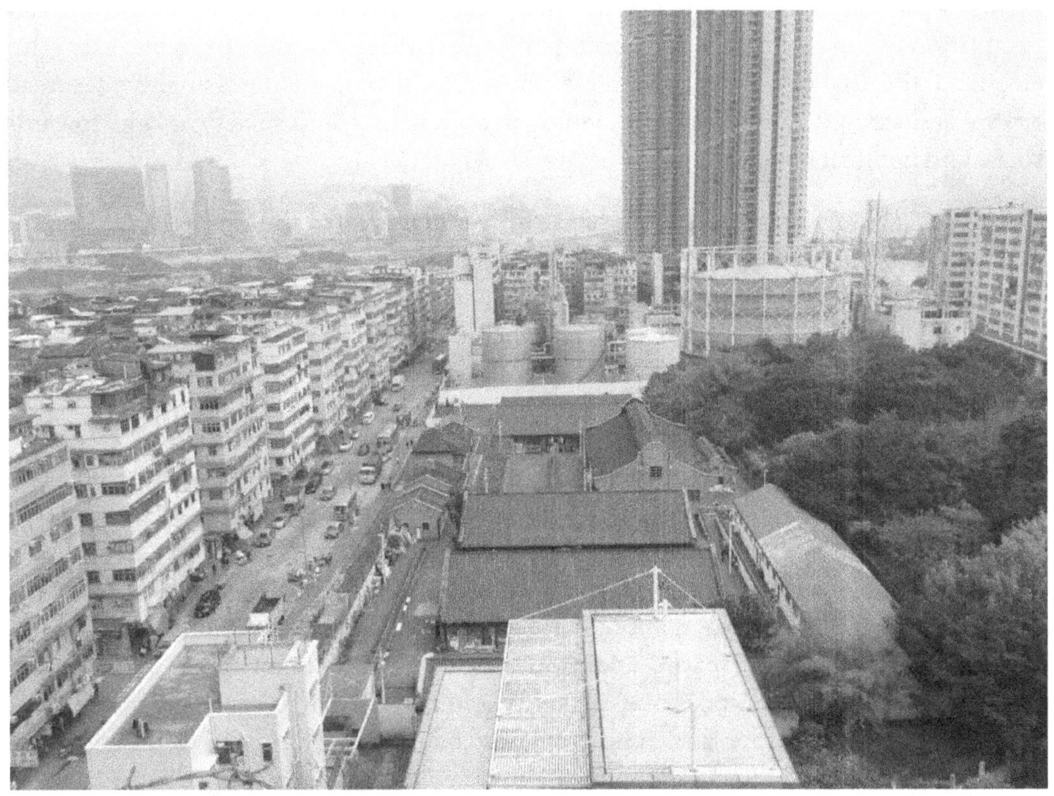

Photo 2. Opposite to our project space is a sixty-year-old neighbourhood of around eighty eight-storey buildings, where low-income families from ethnic minorities and newcomers from Mainland China are located.

Our mission is to inspire and motivate people to be creative and imaginative by sharing new ways of play, and to explore the potential for socially engaged art practice as a vehicle to generate new collaborations and social cohesion. A rolling artist-in-residence programme is held at our space, each taking a different theme and artistic approach. Every season, a resident artist is invited to work for three months in collaboration with the community to transform the space into a new playground.

Through different open-ended arts programmes, we encourage young people, parents, and children to invent their own creative playthings from waste materials collected from the area, such as wooden plywood pallets, abandoned tyres, used clothing, and recycled paper. We bring together artists, artisans, children, parents, and youth to exchange their skills, knowledge, and experiences with each other (Photo 3).

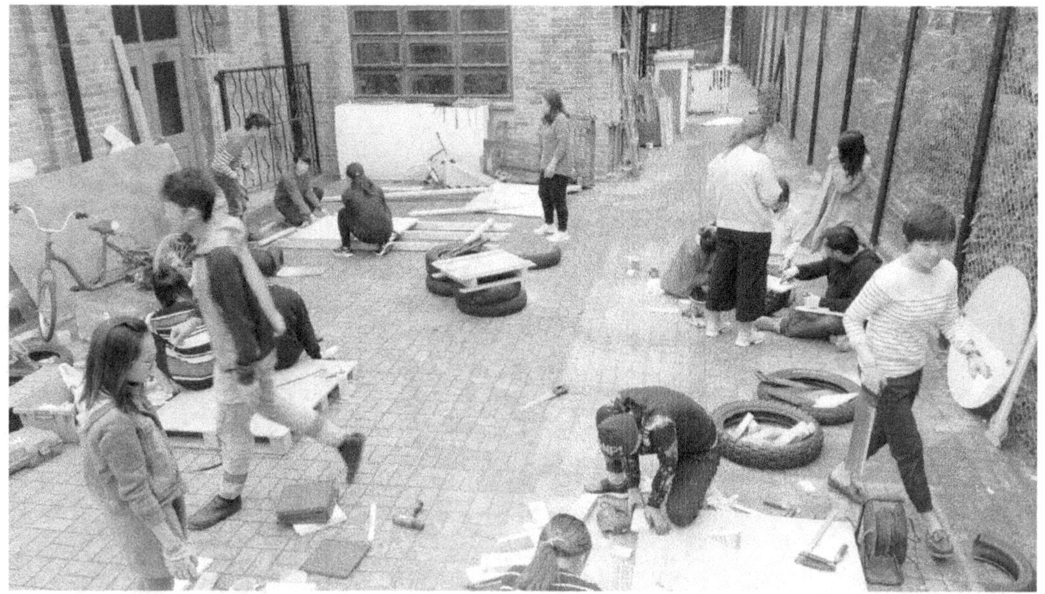

Photo 3. Play Depot works to transform underutilized public spaces into community playgrounds where people can create something on their own and unleash their creativity and aspires to create a socially inclusive space through co-creation approaches.

When children and their families come to the space, they can direct their own imaginative play by experimenting with different materials and play objects, discovering new creative processes in a socially mediated learning environment. Interactions across generations, through the passing on of art and craft-making skills from artists and artisans to youngsters, are encouraged. Youngsters can apply the skills that they learned to create new toys for children. Partnerships are also a key element of the project. We have developed strong relationships with local community groups, schools, youth centres, and social organizations. Together, we create a caring, creative and convivial environment for all people regardless of age, gender, ethnicity, income, or educational background to share the joy of creativity and socialise without a set agenda. The type of people who come to our space generally include:

Families:

Parents in Hong Kong are very concerned with the physical and emotional wellbeing of their children in an increasingly pressurized education system. Many of them find existing children activities too expensive and not well suited to their individual needs. They always look for different games and activities that are intellectually and physically rewarding to play with their children, and have loads of ideas to make toys from scrap materials for sharing with others.

Children:

Lots of neighbouring children from different backgrounds come to our space. Some are from ethnic minorities, e.g., Muhsan is a kid from the Pakistani community in Hong Kong whose parents are from working class backgrounds living in the neighbouring area. He comes with his younger sister and friends almost every other day (Photo 4).

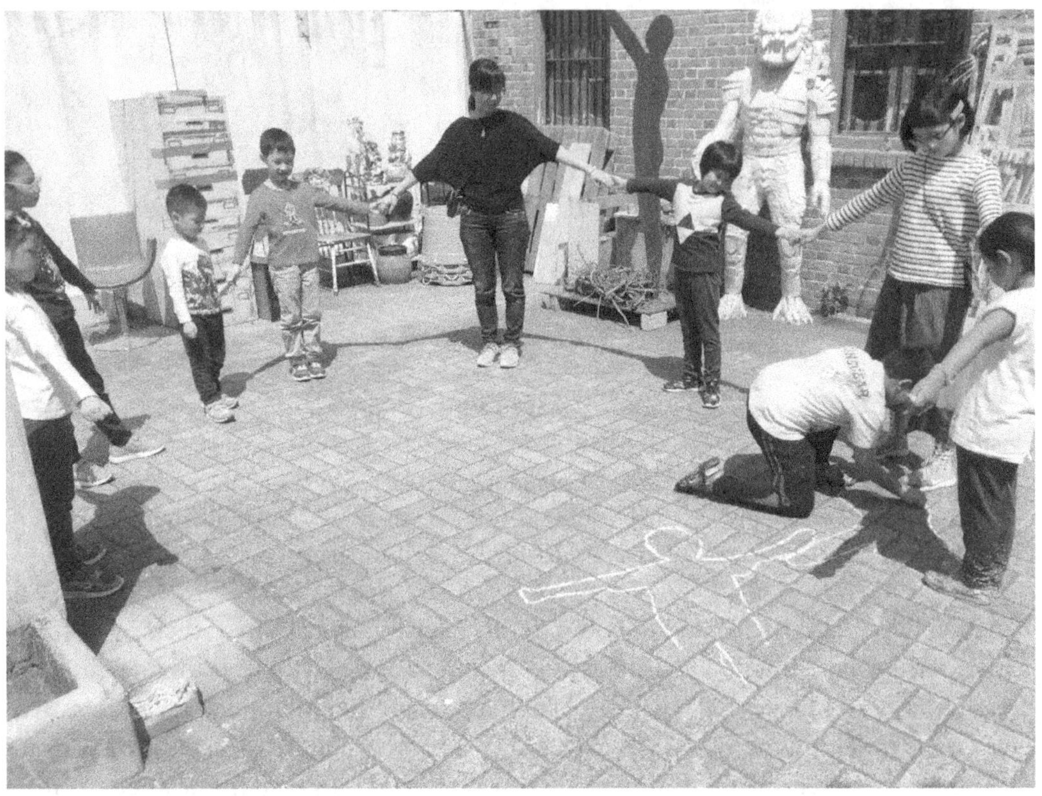

Photo 4. An everyday scene at Play Depot, where artists join the children from the neighbourhood to play and have fun together.

Retirees:

Mr Leung is a retiree who has been living in the neighbouring area for over thirty years. He used to work in a small factory nearby operating hydraulic press machines to press metal and stainless steel into tools. He regards craft as a form of play. He enjoys using scrap wood to design and make chairs that he then gives away.

We believe that play is for everybody. It involves tactile connections among materials, people, and ideas. It inherently has a social dimension, as play increases people's engagements with their social and physical environments. The activities at Play Depot are free flowing, participative, and ever changing in order to counter with the problem of societal consumerist attitudes. Our approach, unlike those of other organisations engaging public audiences with arts and culture, is not from a consumption point of view. As Barnard

(2004) states, "people have become divorced from authentic experience, are passive spectators of their own lives and no longer communicate or participate in the society of spectacle. The dominant form of spectacular commodity production and consumption ensures that people do not engage in self-directed or autonomous activity, but answer the needs of the spectacle." The focus of our activities is to offer different forms of authentic experiences and proactive behaviours.

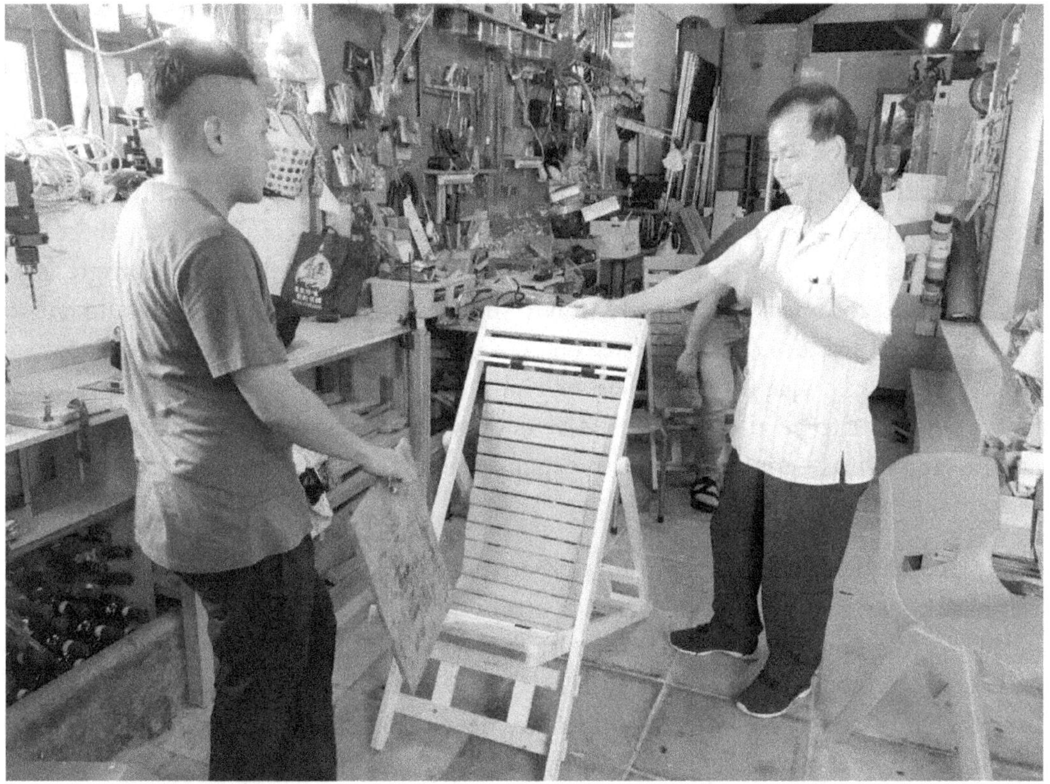

Photo 5. Mr Leung, a retired factory technician living in the area for over thirty years, generously brings love and care to the community by giving people a place to rest with his handmade wooden lounge chairs, thanks to his great craftwork skills.

Huizinga (1955) reminds us at the beginning of his book *Homo Ludens* that "all play is a voluntary activity" and so "play to order is no longer play." He then emphasizes the idea of play as an act of freedom that is bounded. It entails a set of rules and responsibilities underpinned by an ethic of fair play. This is evident from a quote from him:

> Civilization will, in a sense, always be played according to certain rules, and true civilization will always demand fair play. Fair play is nothing less than good faith expressed in play terms. Hence the cheat or the spoil-sport shatters civilization itself. To be a sound culture-creating force this play-element must be pure. It must not consist in the darkening or debasing of standards set up by reason, faith or humanity. It

> must not be a false seeming, a masking of political purposes behind the illusion of genuine play-forms. True play knows no propaganda; its aim is in itself, and its familiar spirit is happy inspiration. (Huizinga 1955)

His book not only lucidly unfolds the meanings of play, but also sheds new light on its pivotal roles and functions in shaping various aspects of our cultures and thus civilization of society. It articulates the virtues and criteria that need to be cultivated deep in the hearts of everyone in order for a just and civilized society to be sustained.

At the heart of play is the high degree of freedom that we have to shape our own lives and the world around us. Flanagan (2009) gives us the best description of play in this context. In her book *Critical Play: Radical Game Design*, she defines play "as a process of signification, play traverses ordinary life and allows players to take on difficult issues from an insulated position." It is known that play is essential to children's growth, cognitive development, and socialisation. It is also commonly agreed that play is progressive, engaging, and communal. But in addition to that, through this project, we would like to contribute towards building resilience and common good with the community that we serve, particularly with those who do not have easy access to play or traditionally not been considered to be involved in creative endeavours. A key aspect of this project is to employ an inclusive approach so as to expand the target group to include participants, making the group as diverse as possible.

Many people tend to think themselves too small to make a difference to the society, let alone collectively to enact a shared common goal. Of course, the complexity of the problems that our societies and humanity face is beyond our comprehension. China's authoritarianism, US right-wing populism, UK's Brexit, and Europe's refugee crisis ... all over the world, most societies have become more polarized. Looking at history of the world, we know that civilization can easily come to a halt in a blink.

But the notion of play makes us think in another way about what we can do. It changes people from being aloof and withdrawn to being proactive and engaged in genuine dialogue. Most people seem to think human beings are an advanced creation. But most do not see that we are still affected by our primal nature.

Despite the fact that we are still primal beings, a brighter side of our innate nature exists —the ability of play that is rooted in human nature and that is not something we need to learn to do. We should exercise more this positive side of our innate ability in order to redefine our limitations and replace negativity with positivity. This innate nature enables us to open up our eyes to possibilities, look for new ways of doing things, and recognise needs in others. Through this innate nature, we cultivate our virtues and train ourselves to be better citizens.

Soon after we embarked on this project, we were successful in enhancing people's access to public spaces through our socially engaged arts practice. We brought together a lot of local residents and neighbours who might not have met each other otherwise. Over the last three years, we have gone further to be a catalyst that empowers the local community regardless of age and background to incite creativity and a spirit of communal support, sharing, and generosity through playfulness activities.

Yet still, in spite of all these efforts, we know that we cannot solve all problems with this tiny project. There seems to be no end in sight to the political and social crisis in Hong Kong. The current situation forces us to acknowledge the fact that our society has become even more polarised. I think it is fair to say that there is a tremendous friction that feeds into further polarisation and the danger of indifference associated with it, as oppose to the counter-narrative that we are bringing about.

I believe in the creative power of arts. It can help people recognise that they can take control of their life and make changes to society. The arts are a precious asset to be shared with all people regardless of their background, which enables us to work more collaboratively. There is still much to do in order to unlock people's desire for the arts and to reach a wider public. All in all, at a critical and uncertain time, play is even more important.

References

Amnesty International Hong Kong. 2019. "Verified: Hong Kong Police Violence Against Peaceful Protesters." June 21, https://www.amnesty.org.hk/en/verified-hong-kong-police-violence-against-peaceful-protesters/.

Barnard, Adam. 2004. "The Legacy of the Situationist International: The Production of Situationists of Creative Resistance." *Capital & Class*: 107

BBC. 2019. "Hong Kong protests: What is the 'Umbrella Movement?'" September 28, https://www.bbc.co.uk/newsround/49862757.

Chan, Holmes. 2019. "'Servants of Triads': Hong Kong democrats Claim Police Condoned Mob Attacks in Yuen Long." *Hong Kong Free Press*, July 22, https://www.hongkongfp.com/2019/07/22/servants-triads-hong-kong-democrats-claim-police-condoned-mob-attacks-yuen-long/.

Cheng, Gary. 2019. "Extradition Bill Crisis: How the Hong Kong Government had the 'Perfect' Listening Mechanisms, but Turned a Deaf Ear to Public Sentiment." *South China Morning Post*, August 14, https://www.scmp.com/news/hong-kong/politics/article/3022657/extradition-bill-crisis-case-study-how-hong-kong-government.

Flanagan, Mary. 2009. *Critical Play: Radical Game Design*. MIT Press.

Haas, Benjamin. 2019. "A Polarized City, Mirrored in Its Diaspora." *The Atlantic*, October 20, https://www.theatlantic.com/international/archive/2019/10/hong-kong-politics-diaspora/600250/

Hernández, Javier, Barbara Marcolini, Haley Willis, Drew Jordan, Meg Felling, Tiffany May, and Elsie Chen. 2009. "Did Hong Kong Police Abuse Protesters? What Videos Show." *New York Times,* June 30, https://www.nytimes.com/2019/06/30/world/asia/did-hong-kong-police-abuse-protesters-what-videos-show.html.

Huizinga, Johan. 1955. *Homo Ludens: A Study of the Play-Element in Culture.* Beacon Press.

Lai, Catherine. 2019. "'Cruel to Both Sides': Hong Kong Protests Divide Neighbourhood With Police Families." *Hong Kong Free Press*, August 12, https://www.hongkongfp.com/2019/08/12/cruel-sides-hong-kong-protests-divide-neighbourhood-police-families/.

Mahtani, Shibani, Timothy McLaughlin, Tiffany Liang, and Ryan Ho Kilpatrick. 2019. "In Hong Kong Crackdown, Police Repeatedly Broke their Own Rules—And Faced No Consequences." *The Washington Post,* December 24, https://www.washingtonpost.com/graphics/2019/world/hong-kong-protests-excessive-force/?fbclid=IwAR1xJ8dFxJaNYiLk81cve94qXvGseDLQx9Pj3QUp9nYAsTf7OGYDwbN_hwI.

Time. 2019. "A Hong Kong Extradition Protester Who Fell to His Death Is Being Hailed as a 'Martyr." June 15, https://time.com/5607742/hong-kong-protester-dies-anti-extradition/?fbclid=IwAR1UdwA8Sw4cHie9FmSHIyYeVBqUIjsYYXvBmD9puCpyHoOVY6g6NLNwl6g.

Yu, Verna, and Lily Kuo. 2019. "Hong Kong: 1.7m People Defy Police to March in Pouring Rain." *The Guardian,* August 18, https://www.theguardian.com/world/2019/aug/18/hong-kong-huge-rally-china-condemns-us-gross-interference

MUSEUMS AND THEIR RELEVANCE IN BORNO STATE, NIGERIA

ZAINAB MUSA SHALLANGWA

University of Maiduguri

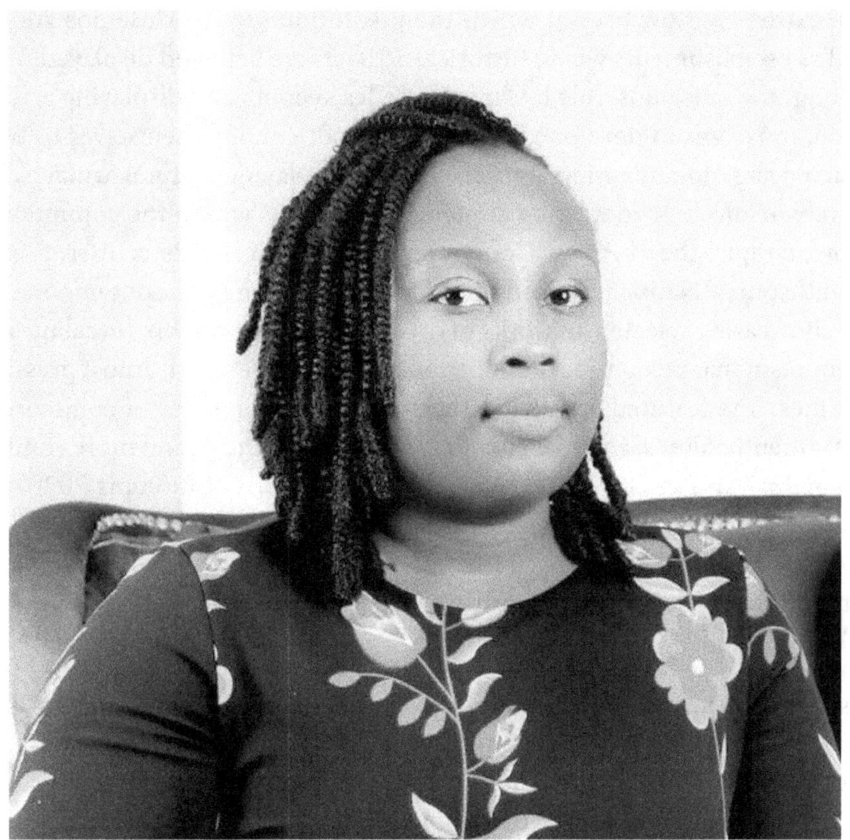

Zainab Musa Shallangwa is lecturer in the Department of Fine Arts of the University of Maiduguri, Borno State, Nigeria. She holds a B.A Degree in Creative Arts (Art History and Museology) from the University of Maiduguri and a Masters Degree in Museums and Heritage Studies from the University of Ghana, Legon. Presently, Zainab is a PhD Student of a Binational Doctoral Degree at the University of Maiduguri (Nigeria) and the University of Hildesheim (Germany) under the SDG-Graduate School "Performing Sustainability. Cultures and Development in West Africa."

INTRODUCTION

Museums are public cultural and educational institutions that occupy an important place in national development. They preserve the tangible and intangible culture of the communities in which they are located, and the public they serve derives benefits and pleasure from their displays. In Borno State, Nigeria, however, there is a question of the relevance of museums, particularly in the present day, given the extremely slow pace at which the institution grows. Museums are generally perceived as establishments where historical artifacts are kept and displayed. While this is not wrong, the museums' role by far supersedes keeping and displaying artifacts. For this reason, museums in developed countries do not confine themselves to traditional roles of acquiring, documenting, conserving and displaying cultural artifacts. They are now actively involved in addressing contemporary issues within the communities they serve. For example, the "I Am ... Contemporary Women Artists of Africa" exhibition of the Smithsonian National Museum of African Art addresses contemporary gender issues by showcasing selected artworks of diverse media by women, revealing a contemporary feminism that recognizes the contributions of women to the most pressing issues of their times. The featured artists use their art to address issues of community, faith, the environment, politics, colonial encounters, racism, identity, and more (Smithsonian Museum of African Art 2019). The Museum Association's "Museums 2020" initiative for the future development of the sector provides further clarification on how museums are expected to benefit society, ranging from "improving people's lives, building communities, strengthening society and protecting the environment" (Museums Association 2012: 3).

The museum as an institution is an important constituent of modern society and if well harnessed, can go a long way in shaping societal progress. Cultural education, the promotion of mutual understanding among ethnic groups in Nigeria, the reactivation of rural handicrafts, and economic growth are some of the ways that museums can contribute to nation-building, as suggested by Afigbo and Okita (1985). However, in Nigeria, as in most African countries, communities where museums are located are yet to fully enjoy the benefits of museums. Makuvaza (2002) argues that in Africa, museums as national institutions were not developed to serve local Africans, but rather to satisfy the curiosities of the elite citizenry. He adds that today, these museums are still inaccessible and not enjoyed by the majority, as they are located in urban areas, and their collections and displays still mirror western concepts.

The Oxford Advanced Learners Dictionary defines relevance as "the fact of being valuable and useful to people in their lives and work." In the context of the museum, relevance is linked to the usefulness of the museum in the lives of people, which can be determined first by the level at which the society patronizes the museum. It is only through patronage that it can be revealed whether the experience adds value or not. The main question in this essay is: are the museum staff fulfilling their roles in order to achieve relevance in Borno society? These roles are clearly defined in the definition of a museum by the International Council of Museums. These roles, considered the traditional roles of museums, are the acquisition, documentation, conservation, and exhibition of artifacts in the interest of the communities they serve.

Borno State, located in Northeast Nigeria, is the worst affected state by the Boko Haram campaign of terror, which resulted in the displacement of over 2 million people. The situation rendered many local government areas (LGAs) in Borno State uninhabitable; hence, the inhabitants fled their places of abode to take refuge in neighboring states and neighboring countries—Niger, Cameroon, and Chad—with the majority being in Maiduguri, the Borno State capital. Most of the people that were forced to escape their villages are placed in Internally Displaced Persons (IDP) camps. The museum as a public, cultural, and educational institution has a lot to offer in such times, but unfortunately, this cannot not be achieved as a result of some challenges plaguing the institution, which are discussed in the ensuing sections of this paper.

The findings of this paper obtained through interviews with Borno State museum and the National Museum staff members and National and Borno State Museums visitors revealed that the museums in Borno State are not yet fulfilling their expected roles within the Borno community; hence, their relevance is at stake. The findings point to the fact that the museums in Borno are struggling to fulfill their traditional roles; therefore, keeping up with current museological practices is yet to be achieved.

The museum staff, curators, directors, conservators, educators, and administrators, who all explained that they would prefer not to be identified within this paper, mentioned a number of challenges impeding them from reaching their full potential.

THE EMERGENCE OF MUSEUMS IN NIGERIA

According to Okonkwo Ivan Emeka (2016), the emergence of museums in Nigeria dates back to pre-Arab and -European times. During these periods, Okonkwo notes that various materials of cultural, religious, and political significance were fashioned and preserved in temples, traditional shrines or in the palaces of kings and chiefs. In pre-colonial museums, persons responsible for preserving and organizing these materials were household heads, priests of shrines, and kings' and chiefs' officers who acted as curators.

However, according to Ekpo Eyo (1994), the birth of conventional museums in Nigeria, like in most African countries, can be traced to the beginning of colonization of African countries by Europe in the late nineteenth century, an era that coincided with the development of connoisseurship and scholarship in museum development in Europe. Eyo notes that the early museum left the typical African in a dilemma, as both Islam and Christianity were widespread in most parts of Africa before the formal declaration of colonization in West Africa. The cultural objects, which needed to be preserved, admired, and studied within the museums introduced by the colonial governments, were thus anti-Islam, anti-Christian, and even anti-colonial. This left the typical African confused, as the museum as an institution became a contradiction, and Africans, in an effort to embrace modern western education and the prestige it conferred, became oblivious and often hostile to the very objects which established them as human beings (Eyo 1994). However, independence brought a new light to African museums. African nationalists looked to museums as a mirror to their new status: a cultural institution that was required to buttress political independence. Latham & Simmons (2014) confirm Eyo's claim that "the national systems of museums in Nigeria has played an important role in defining the culture of post revolution Nigeria (P.141)" Latham and Simmons are probably alluding to post-independence Nigeria. The key point here, however, is that the museum institution is an important component of the socio-political landscape. Almost all of the thirty-six states in Nigeria have a national museum alongside a state-owned museum. National museums are directly financed by the federal government of Nigeria, while state museums are financed by the state government. In addition, the national museum displays artifacts from the entire country, while the state museums focus on artifacts from the state in which they are located.

There are currently two museums in Maiduguri, the Borno State capital: The National Museum, which is directly under the National Commission for Museums and Monuments, and the Borno State Museum, which is under the Borno State Ministry of Information and Culture. Both museums hold in trust material evidence of the Borno people and were vibrant places until about the late nineties, when the institution started experiencing a decline. This was exacerbated by the advent of the Boko Haram insurgency. The Borno State National Museum is located in the Custom area in Maiduguri, where the insurgents had established great control until they were sacked in 2013/14. As a result of the control Boko Haram had around the area, the National Museum was out of operations for quite some time and currently operates skeletally for security reasons. The State Museum, on the other hand, is located in the city center and has remained operational; however, the institution has witnessed a setback in its activities for some years because of the security situation and neglect the institution has suffered on the part of the government, which—according to some museum staff—stemmed from the non-profit nature of the institution. The government may be ignorant of the fact that the museum, while maintaining its non-profit status, has the ability to generate revenue indirectly, for instance through tourism. A lot of revenue can be generated indirectly by the museum via transport, hospitality, and accommodation.

FINDINGS

Low patronage

The museums suffer from low patronage. The staff members mentioned that they rarely have visitors now, unlike fifteen to twenty years ago. Narrating their experiences, some staff of the Borno State Museum and the National museum in Maiduguri mentioned:

86

> In the past the museum was a vibrant place, we had visitors from all walks of life- the University, Colleges of Education within Borno State, secondary school students even expatriates because of how well organized and attractive our collections were but we rarely have visitors these days. People hardly remember we exist. We ran shifts on weekends and people had to queue to buy tickets. Today, we can spend a whole week without anyone passing by. (National Museum Maiduguri staff member, April 2019)

> The museum is a shadow of itself today. If anyone had told me this place would be disserted this way some years back, I would not have believed it. Occasionally people visit but the truth is the number of visitors has dropped drastically. The issue of underfunding has affected our outlook seriously. (Borno State Museum staff member, April 2019)

Poor Structure and Infrastructure

The museums' buildings are in bad shape and require renovation. This has an effect on the collections. The museums lack adequate equipment to control the temperature. Holes in the walls allow dust to settle on the objects, threatening their longevity. Talking about poor structure and infrastructure, a staff member said:

> We lack the adequate equipment to preserve our collections that is why we are losing them. The place is poorly maintained too. This makes it impossible for us to fulfill our mandate of preserving these artifacts for posterity. (April 2019)

Unqualified Staff

Most of the museum staff lack knowledge of standard museological practices and are therefore not concerned about this malfunction.

> Most of the staff here have no background in museology that is why our collections are in this state. They do not feel passionate about the state of these artifacts. (Borno State Museum staff member, April 2019)

Low Funding

Museum staff members complained that lack of government funding is a major challenge and impedes their efficiency. The decline in the number of visitors has greatly impacted their work as well. They are expected to make use of these funds to maintain their collections, structure, and infrastructure since the institution is non-profit, but this has become almost impossible.

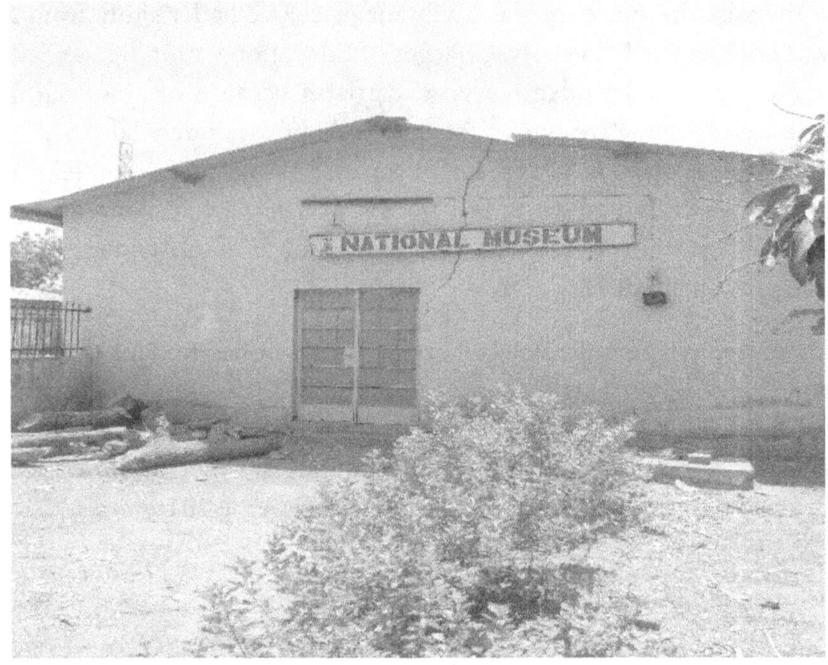

Plate 1. National Museum Building, Maiduguri. (Source: Author, 2019.)

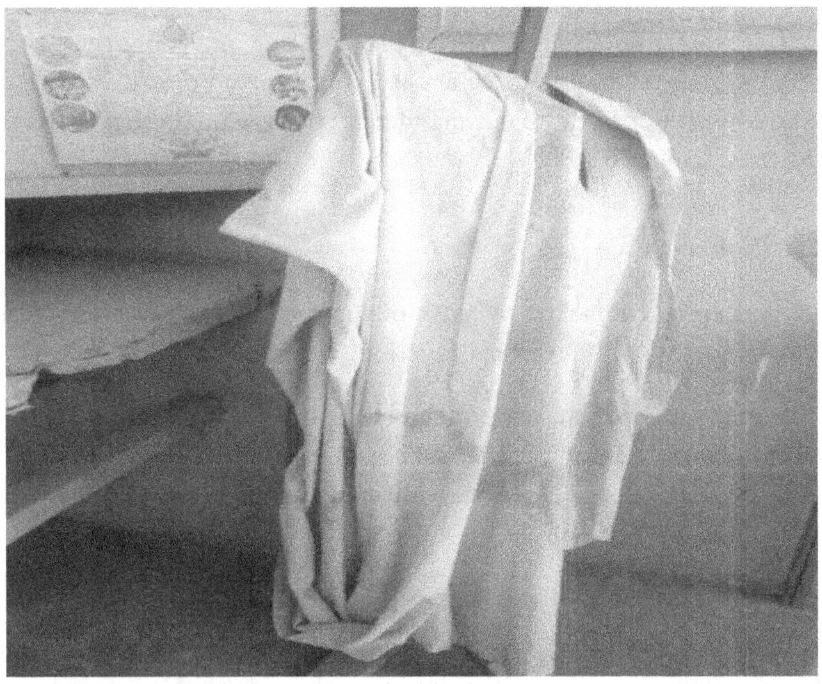

Plate 2. Traditional Borno male garment, National Museum Maiduguri exhibit. (Source: Author, 2019.)

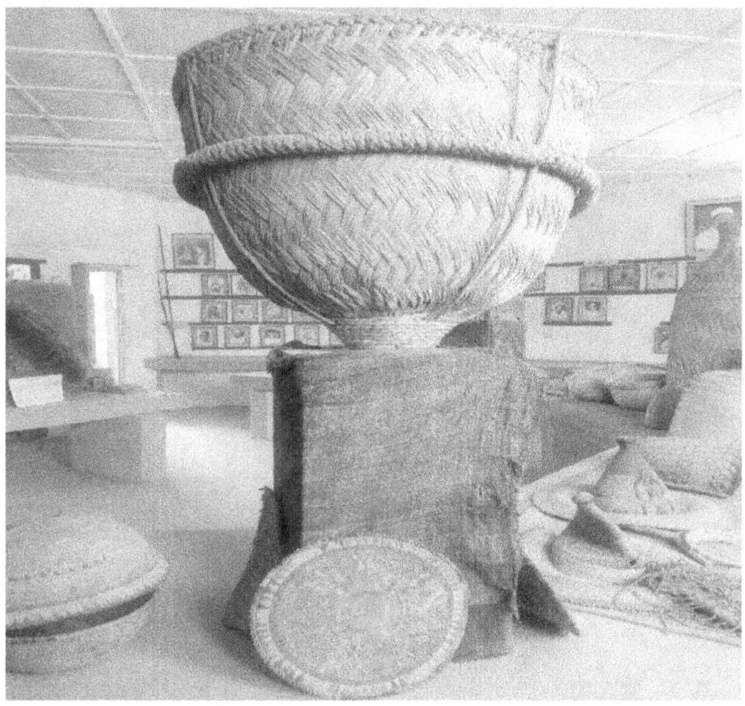

Plate 3. Traditional Raffia products, Borno State Museum Exhibit. (Source: Author, 2019.)

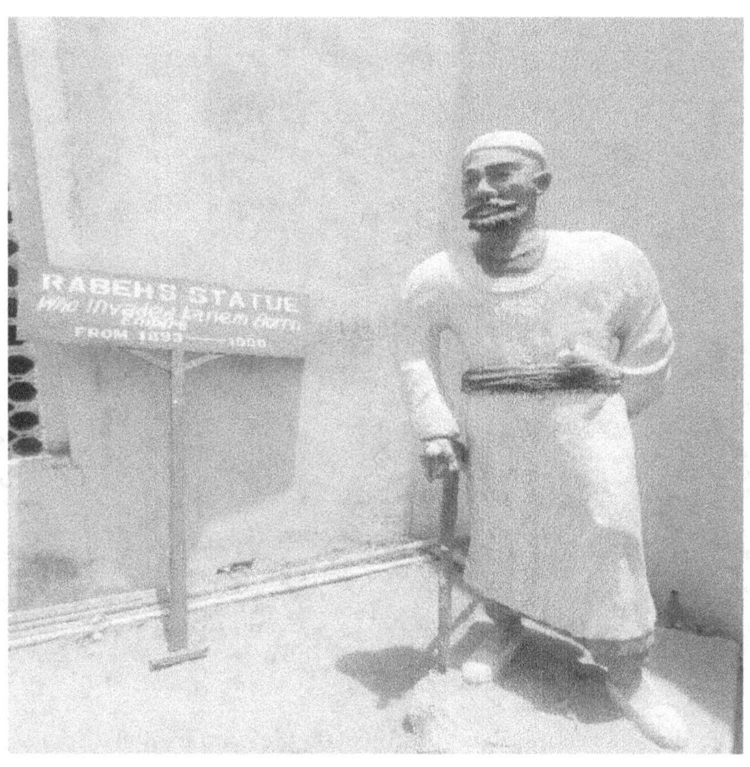

Plate 4. Rabeh's statue, Borno State Museum Courtyard. (Source: Author, 2019.)

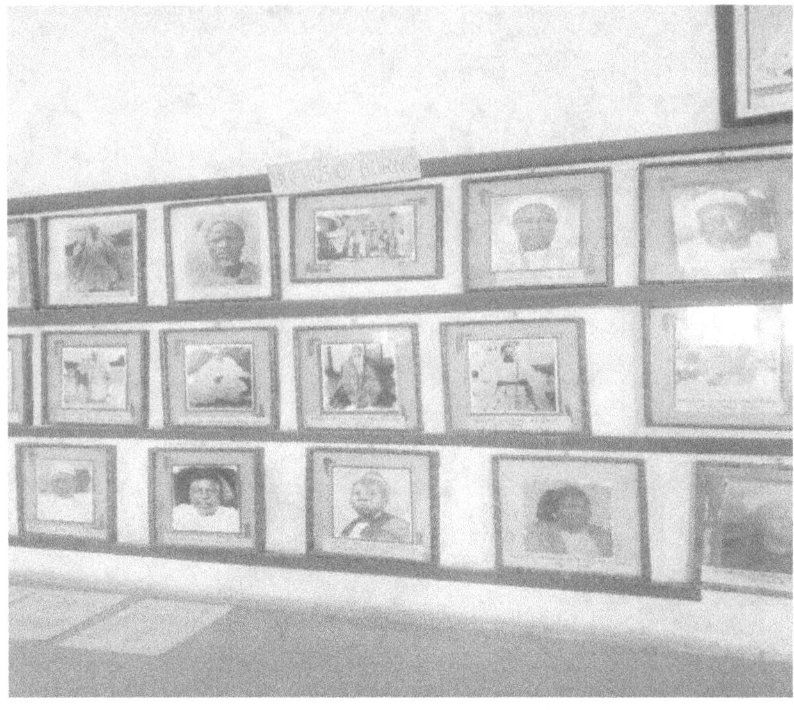

Plate 5. Past traditional leaders of Borno, State Museum Exhibit. (Source: Author, 2019.)

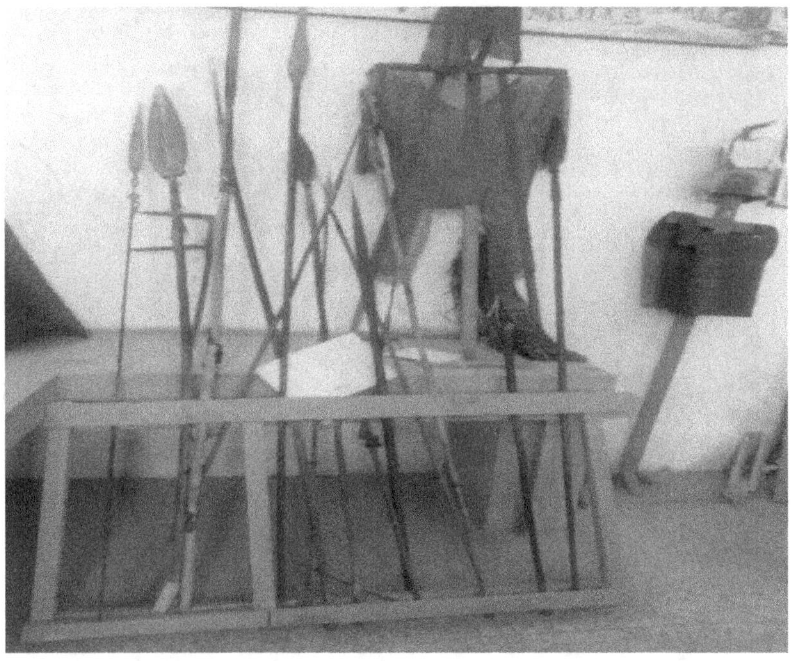

Plate 6. Traditional war implements, Borno State Museum Exhibit. (Source: Author.)

> Because of the low patronage, we cannot fund ourselves. We need more financial support from the government and other organizations. The annual funding hardly gets to us. Recently, we collaborated with North East Regional Initiative (NERI) on a project. We went to several IDP camps enlightening the people about our cultural values and it was a huge success. Such collaborations and support will go a long way in helping us fulfill our mandate. (Borno State Museum staff member, April 2019)

> I am a trained museologist and I am familiar with standard museological practices but the truth is there is almost nothing we can do without adequate funding. Once the funding is there, we are able and willing to work. (National Museum staff member, Maiduguri, April 2019)

A museum visitor narrating her experience after a guided tour of the Borno State Museum explained:

> I enjoyed the tour, it was very educative. I learnt a lot about the past today. (April 2019)

Another female visitor to the museum said:

> My brother was here last week and he encouraged me to visit. I like the cultural artifacts on display. (April 2019)

The Borno society has a lot to benefit from the museums in the state, especially in the era of insurgency and displacement. For instance, the Borno State Museum has a wide range of cultural artifacts from displaced communities within the state; the museum space could help these people stay in touch with their cultures, which could have therapeutic effects, as the IDPs are traumatized. Further, their displacement has lingered for about five years. This implies that a number of children have been born who have never been to their place of origin; the museum becomes overly relevant in telling the stories about their home to these young children. The museums are reference points for a wide range of issues; hence, efforts must be made in order to ensure the relevance and sustainability of these institutions in Borno State and the country at large.

RECOMMENDATIONS

It is important for the Borno state museums to become fully operational, as their benefits for society cannot be overstated. It is a reference point for a wide range of cultural, social, historical, and economical issues, among others. To achieve this, I recommend the following to the Borno State government:

- Upgrade the facility by renovating the building and installing necessary equipment to prevent further deterioration of the objects.

- Encourage museum staff to come up with new programs to improve the public patronage of the museum.

- Ensure the training of museum staff on standard museological practices by funding trainings and workshops. This can also be possible through collaborations and partnerships with universities and other educational institutions like the Institute for Archaeology and Museum Studies, Jos, Plateau State, Nigeria.

- Encourage educational institutions at all levels to partner with the museum to benefit from the information and leisure the museum offers.

The museum staff also have to play a part in ensuring the sustainability and relevance of the museum institution. They need to do the following:

- Staff members should key into strategies of more established museums and museum groups around the world and adapt their strategies for sustainability. For example, the UK Museum Association's agenda, "Museums 2020," is a strategy that aims to make museums more useful as social institutions and more relevant in the context of the twenty-first century. The museums in Borno can learn from such strategies and adapt the relevant parts that fit the Borno society. This will go a long way in keeping the institution relevant.

- Since a number of museum staff members have a background in museology, they should invest in drafting robust programs that will attract support and funding. This will help the museum regain its lost glory.

- Staff members also need to partner with other museums across the globe. This will bring a great deal of improvement in services, thereby making the institution more relevant.

There is also a need to incorporate Afrocentric ideals into the philosophy, operations, and modus operandi of museums across the African continent. For instance, the idea of who exactly constitutes an expert in the service of a museum needs to be reappraised from an Africanist orientation. Local populations should be brought in by museums in Africa, rather than these museums being overly reliant on university scholars and supposedly expert curators. Locals will therefore have a sense of ownership and relate more with the museum. Anah Cletus Ikecukwu (2014) argues that as a colonial construct, Nigerian museums have been confined to the role of tourist attraction. He further argues that the cultural artifacts on display in Nigerian museums symbolize history, belief systems, achievements, values, ideas about human dignity, and so on. He suggests a radical overhaul and reorientation of the museum itself for the institution to reach its full potential.

CONCLUSION

Conventional museums have essentially remained unprogressive, poorly patronized, and seriously underfunded in Nigeria. The institution is barely recognized even by the government. The fact that the institution generates little or no income for the government is probably responsible for the neglect on the part of the government. The Eurocentric ideals upon which the museum institution was established in Africa, as opined by Makuvaza (2002), and the unprogressive nature of museums in the country are probable factors as well. All hope is not lost though, as this can be corrected by injecting some of the recommendations presented in this article. Museums in Borno have the potential of achieving success that would bring needed adjustments towards the realization of relevance and sustainability of the institution. A rise in the number of visitors and the level of community participation/involvement in museum programs and activities are strong indictors of these successes.

REFERENCES

Afigbo, Adiele Eberechukwu, and Silas Ibu O. Okita, eds. 1995. *The Museum and Nation Building*. Owerri: New Africa Publishing Company Ltd.

Anah, Cletus Ikecukwu. 2014. "Repositioning the Museum in Nigeria for Social Change and Sustainable Development." *International Journal of Education and Research* 2 (11): 545–54.

Eyo, Ekpo. 1994. "Conventional Museums and the Quest for Relevance in Africa." *History in Africa* 21: 325–337.

Hornby, Albert Sydney. 1995. *Oxford Advanced Learner's Dictionary of Current English*. Oxford, England: Oxford Univeristy Press.

Letham, Kiersten F., and John E. Simmons Foundation. 2014. *Foundation of Musuems Studies: Evolving Sysytem of knowlwdge*. Santa Barbara: Libraries Unlimited.

Makuvaza, Simon. 2002. *Towards a New Type of 'Ethnographic' Museum in Africa*, https://www.researchgate.net/publication/301815606_Towards_a_new_type_of_%27ethnographic%27_museum_in_Africa.

Museums Association. 2012. *Musuems 2020 Discussion Paper*. https://www.museums association.org/download?id=806530.

Okonkwo, Emeka I. 2016. "Museum Education in Nigeria: Prospects and Challenges." *IGWEBUIKE: An African Journal of Arts and Humanities* 2 (6): 19–39.

Smithsonian National Museum of African Art. 2019. *Current Exhibitions*. https://africa.si.edu/exhibitions/current-exhibitions/.

WHEN INTERCULTURAL LEARNING AND DEMOCRACY MEET IN MUSIC: WHAT NEXT?

QINHAN CHEN
University of Edinburgh

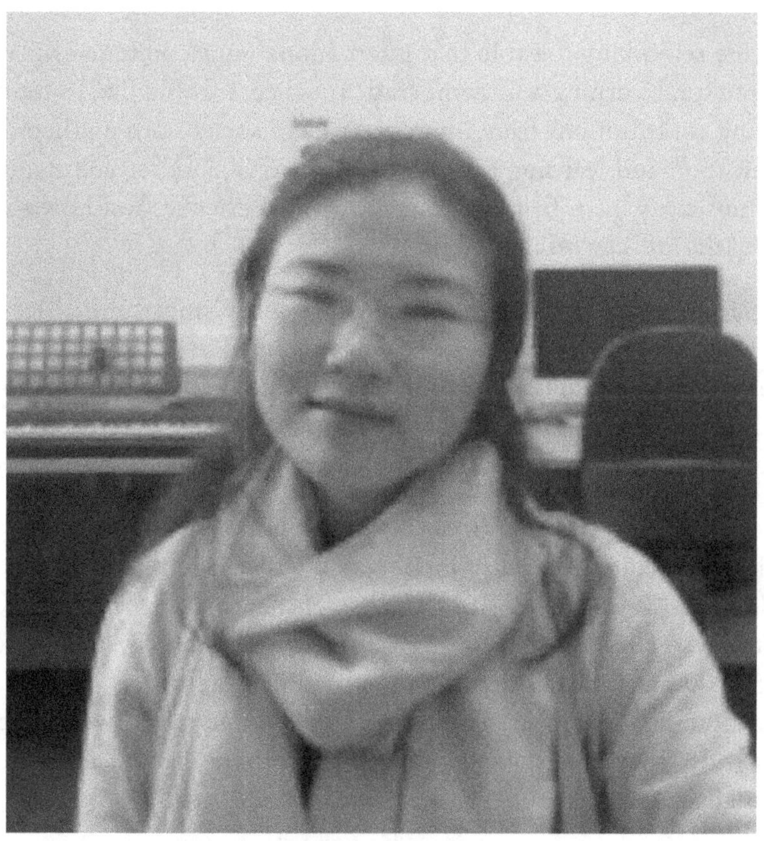

Qinhan Chen is a Ph.D candidate at the University of Edinburgh (UK). She is a member of the Institute for Music in Human and Social Development (IMHSD). She studied Intercultural Communication for masters' degree at the University of Warwick, and her current research focuses on issues of communication, learning, and identity in musicians' practice across intercultural and music domain. Beyond her research interests, she has been dedicated to coordinating music and intercultural events (e.g. Bilingual Ceilidh, Music Across Borders Project, etc.), facilitating local interactions between cultural communities in Scotland.

Classical music communities were shaken when news broke of the controversial leadership style of Daniel Barenboim, the renowned conductor and co-founder of West-Eastern Divan Orchestra (WEDO). With his international career and well-intentioned facilitation of intergroup understanding between Israeli and Palestinian people (Ramel et al. 2018), he is expected to possess and show empathy rather than callousness and even tyrant-like behaviour, as described in the latest reports (Marshall et al. 2019).

Many might be rethinking the role that international music initiatives play in an individual's intercultural learning and democratic practice. I would like to touch upon this question, using contributions from intercultural and social learning theories. Focusing on communication and learning processes that involve another culture, it is essential to ask how musicians learn from an intercultural experience, and how the process of democratising the arts can be a part of it.

First, do musicians learn from intercultural experiences? Intercultural learning entails that operational, affective, and cognitive changes happen in sustained social interaction with people of another cultural group (Kim 2001). Numerous music collaborations have professionals of different cultures work together in one-off and long-term projects. However, these do not automatically result in such learning or in democratic development.

For instance, it has been observed that less communication and learning takes place if people of the same cultural group function as a buffer. Such a contrast is shown in a 1994 PBS documentary, *Between Two Cultures: Japanese in America,* which follows small groups of Japanese families who live in Georgetown, Kentucky and New York City, which has 56,000 Japanese residents. In international orchestras like WEDO, having co-nationals around can help musicians avoid most interactions with other members. However, provided there is sustained intercultural communication, even on a minimum level, they still learn (Kim 2001).

Democratic practice and understanding in this context can be associated with, but is not tantamount to, being open to individuals of different groups in practice and to their opinions in meaning negotiation (Wenger 1998). It can be illustrated by two interviews of Kourelou, a London-based Greek band. Elisavet Sotiriadou at *fRoots Magazine* described their performance: "no instrument stands above any other and no musician is more important than any other. Each of them brings in any influences, feeling and interpretation they have to the songs they play." In another interview with Lida Aslanidou at *New Diaspora,* their violinist Nikos Kyrios stated:

> I always wanted to bring the epirotic element to Kourelou—Epirus is the Greece I carry within me. I don't want to insult the variety of Greek sounds, the traditional music from the islands, from Macedonia, from the Peloponnese, Crete or Pontus, but my priority was to add the epirotic element to Kourelou—Pavlos immediately embraced it!

Although Kourelou's members are all from Greece, their backgrounds are more diverse than the single Greek category under which they are often sorted. From the same country or not, cultural boundaries are revealed to individuals whenever they experience discontinuity and unfamiliarity in interactions (Akkerman et al. 2011). It is the same for musicians whose parent(s) migrated to another country—they were raised and live between different cultures at home and outside (Georgoulas et al. 2017). Their practice may inform professionals in arts management, cultural and social policy, and international education, addressing integration challenges faced by many societies.

How do people learn from intercultural experience? In Communities of Practice theory, Wenger (1998) suggests that people participate and persist in a practice when they feel it is central to their self-efficacy and envisioned identity. In this case, it is to be a great musician/person. Social participation is essential to reaching those aims through learning and identity negotiation, through which one acquires competencies as to ways to interact, think, and feel like an insider (e.g., to become a traditional or jazz musician, or to be Chinese or Scottish). More importantly, such a social history of learning makes it a priceless resource for future identification and negotiation.

Similar to intercultural learning, functional fitness like acoustic adjustments (e.g., tuning and volume) makes learning requirements to be confronted and solved for musical collaborations explicit (Kim 2001). I do not intend to focus on musical techniques here, but instead on parallel communication and its learning mechanism. An operational *sine qua non*, going from language to improvisation skills may be an arduous learning task; nonetheless, it is easier to spot than nuanced understandings like implicit value systems (Shaules 2007).

As social interaction is a central aspect of learning, Wenger proposes three types of boundary encounters: one-on-one, immersion, and delegation. In one-on-one interactions like duo projects, learning happens on an individual level, similar to international couples in which one adapts slightly to the other. In an immersive boundary encounter, such as when musicians go abroad on their own or play as a guest in another ensemble, learning often falls on them. Bands can also exist in the form of a delegation, like how members of Ney Anban (Iran) and Assynt (Scotland) were brought together at Celtic Connections and collaborated. If musicians find their music compatible during encounters, a boundary practice like Afro Celt Sound System might be crystallised and maintained, and intercultural communication and learning take place.

Intercultural communication results in learning and adaptation over time, but not necessarily in democracy. This brings us to the second question: how can democratising the arts be a part of intercultural learning?

One particular individual or group often has more influence over an intergroup project. Having abundant international experience working with people from different cultural groups, Barenboim's leadership style appears to be less than ideal, even though he endeavoured to achieve Israeli-Palestine reconciliation through WEDO. Cultural critics also note that despite Peter Gabriel and Paul Simon's best intentions, hidden socioeconomic inequality hindered their international projects, with one side taking a central role and the other enjoying no say in decisions or acknowledgements (Frith 1996; Taylor 1997).

Democratic practice does not always encourage intercultural development either. When there is no spark (as there rarely is), communication and mutual learning are required in order for creative solutions to emerge. It is natural for individuals to cling to familiar relations, practices, perspectives, and opinions (Wenger 1998). From international festivals to orchestras, it is reasonable to observe "dialogue between diverse partners established only as far as necessary to maintain the flow of work" (Akkerman et al. 2011, 143). Dropping musicians into a new cultural group in collaboration or new environment on a trip can be stressful and cannot guarantee democracy. Their opinion may not immediately be taken into account by the hosts; however, collaboration effectively engages them in cultural learning.

On certain occasions, musicians seem to perceive democratic practice as essential for engagement. First, when musical communities negotiated democracy as professional behaviour in creating meaningful work, adapting to each other is deemed necessary for the music-making process. Becker (2000, 172) remarks, as a pianist and sociologist, how seemingly free-form jazz improvisation is an "aggressively egalitarian" value and practice. The same etiquette was present in collaboration between traditional ensembles and jazz bands (like Cairo Steps and Quadro Nuevo's Flying Carpet concert). While it is observed that members might not share same understanding in improvisation (Wilson et al. 2012), this arrangement holds every musician accountable, keeps negotiations open, musically and interculturally. On other occasions individuals may value democracy in music because it has been developed as a meaningful engagement as personal identification. In a broadcast interview, Chung Yufeng (2018) mentions that although her pipa sounded too scratchy in a sample mixed by Indonesian sound engineers, she kept it that way as a way to respect their decision.

This shifts us from the operational aspect to understandings that motivate and possibly change with musicians' boundary practices and learning. When advocating music's significance, many may contend that music transcends cultural differences. Individuals recognise cultural differences and their significance, yet think there are some overriding rules. Bennett (1993) has summarised two kinds of reasoning for experiences of cultural similarities: physical universalism based on shared biology and transcendental universalism based on psychological or sociological imperatives.

Admittedly, music transcendental universalism cannot address every cultural conflict, but music provides a ubiquitous practice across cultural boundaries (Hallam et al. 2014). These enable individuals to enjoy their desired outcomes, bypassing language barriers in the short term; some even turn toward a lasting intercultural career. Scholars across disciplines have highlighted the ability to recognise cultural differences, to develop multiple perspectives and consistent self-identification out of incongruent expectations from communities in which individuals feel invested and to which they are held accountable (Berry 2005; Bhabha 2012; Hall 1989; Sparrow 2000; Ward et al. 2001).

In brief, intercultural and democratic understandings are developed in sustained practice wherever individuals find learning necessary and meaningful, experiencing different, yet valid and valuable cultural expectations. It can be seen in Barenboim's talks regarding his concerns and reflections on intergroup conflicts, and in Chung's retrospection on her choices of keeping Indonesian sound engineers' work the way it is. Their developments happen not overnight, but slowly, day-to-day, over the decades.

Over time, shared practice constitutes a shared history irreplaceable for an imagination mechanism, as Anderson (2006) suggests, which binds a society together through members envisaging a shared past and future. Moving from individual to societal foci, intercultural incidents grow with the ethnic composition shift in many countries (van Oudenhoven et al. 2015). Such intercultural experiences in domestic societies are a key factor for learning (Harrison 2012). Consequent mutual accommodations have been observed in the pluralist societies that have a relatively high proportion of minority communities, despite their separate interests (Haugen et al. 2017). Similarly, a shared sense of history cultivated at WEDO—even if limited—lead its members to rent accommodations on the same street in Berlin despite their national conflicts (Riiser 2010).

Mass migrations over the decades have resulted in many musicians' professional and personal learning being furthered by intercultural experience, despite feeling chasms between their musical and cultural belongings. Those conflicted feelings are expressed in published accounts by renowned Anoushka Shankar, Japanese American musician Kaoru Watanabe, who was born and raised in St. Louis, among others (Grillo 2016). The topic also attracted research interest by Greek Australian musician Calista, who was born to Greek parents and raised in Melbourne (Georgoulas et al. 2017), and Steve Kapur, the "Apache Indian" English-born Punjabi musician (Lipsitz 1994). One way people learnt to bring together various practices and identities is to allow all cultures and all people to contribute and be a part of a community, musically and culturally (Kim 2001).

From a social identity perspective, this music-cultural association is a reification resulting from constant social negotiations between what individuals and communities value: separate cultural identities, integrated group practice, individualised expressions, dialogues, and/or hybrid projects. There is not one, but plural answers: William James (1974) suggests that truth is subjective and a self-contained description of the world. In order to see to sustained democratic and intercultural rapport as one of the answers, sustainable practice and meaningful experience must be available, and must be related to the personhood pursued by individuals. Egalitarian music-making conventions are as crucial as identity aspirations that enable individuals to envision greater possibilities and meaning for musical and cultural boundary practices.

If nothing else, music collaboration across cultures provides a shared reality for people to develop an intercultural and democratic identity. It is shown in and negotiated through collaborative work like *History 101* between the Native American group SongCatchers and African American musician Charles Neville (Taylor 1997), in *Siwa* between the Indonesian group SambaSunda and Han Taiwanese musician Chung Yufeng, and in groups like Salsa Celtica and Yo-Yo Ma's initiative Silk Road Ensemble, among others. Wenger (1998) highlights the fact that learning cannot be designed but can be designed for; eventually, it is up to each individual and community to develop and negotiate mutual practice, understandings, and shared histories to which they hold dear.

REFERENCES

Akkerman, Sanne F., and Arthur Bakker. 2011. "Boundary Crossing and Boundary Objects." *Review of Educational Research* 81 (2): 132–69.

Anderson, Benedict. 2006. *Imagined Communities: Reflections on the Origin and Spread of Nationalism.* London; New York: Verso books.

Aslanidou, Lida. n.d. "Kourelou in London." *New Diaspora* (blog). Accessed January 14, 2020. http://www.newdiaspora.com/kourelou/.

Becker, Howard S. 2000. "The Etiquette of Improvisation." *Mind, Culture, and Activity* 7 (3): 171–76. https://doi.org/10.1207/S15327884MCA0703_03.

Bennett, Milton J. 1993. "Towards Ethnorelativism: A Developmental Model of Intercultural Sensitivity." In *Education for the Intercultural experience,* edited by R Michael Paige, 2nd ed., 21-71. Yarmouth, Me: Intercultural Press, 1993.

Berry, John W. 2005. "Acculturation: Living Successfully in Two Cultures." *International Journal of Intercultural Relations* 29 (6): 697–712.

Bhabha, Homi K. 2012. *The Location of Culture.* London; New York: Routledge.

Georgoulas, Renee, and Jane E Southcott. 2017. "The 'Bitter Sweetness' of Hybridity: Being a Bicultural Greek Australian Musician." *The Qualitative Report* 22 (6): 1511–24.

Grillo, Tyran. 2016. "Kaoru Watanabe: A RootsWorld Interview." *Rootsworld,* http://www.rootsworld.com/interview/watanabe-16.shtml.

Hall, Edward Twitchell. 1989. *Beyond Culture.* New York: Doubleday.

Hallam, Susan, Ian Cross, Michael Thaut, Susan Hallam, and Raymond MacDonald. 2014. *The Effects of Music in Community and Educational Settings.* Oxford: Oxford

University Press. https://www.oxfordhandbooks.com/view/10.1093/oxfordhb/97 80198722946.001.0001/oxfordhb-9780198722946-e-46.

Harrison, Neil. 2012. "Investigating the Impact of Personality and Early Life Experiences on Intercultural Interaction in Internationalised Universities." *International Journal of Intercultural Relations* 36 (2): 224–37. https://doi.org/10.1016/j.ijintrel.2011.03.007.

Haugen, I., and J.R. Kunst. 2017. "A Two-Way Process? A Qualitative and Quantitative Investigation of Majority Members' Acculturation." *International Journal of Intercultural Relations* 60 (September): 67–82. https://doi.org/10.1016/j.ijintrel.2017.07.004.

James, William. 1974. *Pragmatism: And Four Essays from The Meaning of Truth.* New York: New American Library.

Kim, Young Yun. 2001. *Becoming Intercultural: An Integrative Theory of Communication and Cross-Cultural Adaptation.* Thousand Oaks, Calif: SAGE.

Lipsitz, George. 1994. *Dangerous crossroads: popular music, postmodernism, and the poetics of place.* London: Verso.

Marshall, Alex, and Christopher F. Schuetze. 2019. "Daniel Barenboim Seemed Untouchable. Now He's Accused of Bullying." *The New York Times,* February 26, 2019, https://www.nytimes.com/2019/02/26/arts/music/daniel-barenboim-conductor-bullying-berlin.html.

Ramel, Frédéric, and Michael Jung. 2018. "The Barenboim Case: How to Link Music and Diplomacy Studies." *Arts and International Affairs,* October. https://doi.org/doi:10.18278/aia.3.2.5.

Riiser, Solveig. 2010. "National Identity and the West-Eastern Divan Orchestra." *Music and Arts in Action* 2 (2): 19–37.

Shaules, Joseph. 2007. *Deep Culture: The Hidden Challenges of Global Living.* Clevedon: Multilingual Matters.

Sparrow, Lise M. 2000. "Beyond Multicultural Man: Complexities of Identity." *International Journal of Intercultural Relations* 24 (2): 173–201.

Taylor, Timothy Dean. 1997. *Global Pop: World Music, World Markets.* New York: Routledge.

Ward, Colleen A., Stephen Bochner, and Adrian Furnham. 2001. *The psychology of culture shock.* Hove, East Sussex: Routledge.

Wenger, Etienne. 1998. *Communities of Practice: Learning, Meaning, and Identity.* Cambridge: Cambridge University Press.

Wilson, Graeme B., and Raymond A.R. MacDonald. 2012. "The Sign of Silence: Negotiating Musical Identities in an Improvising Ensemble." *Psychology of Music* 40 (5): 558–73. https://doi.org/10.1177/0305735612449506.

ON THE ROPES

KHALED BARAKEH
Artist

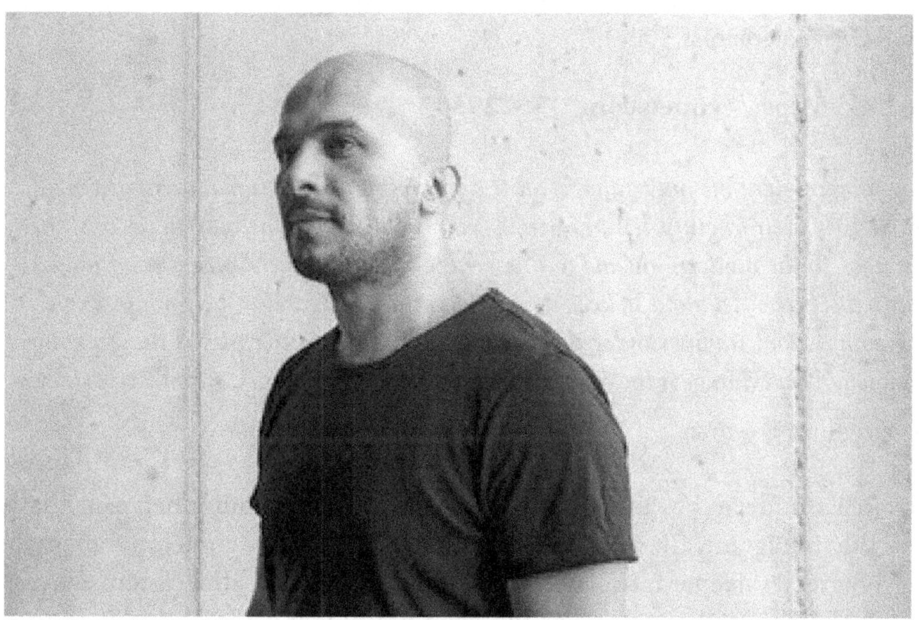

Khaled Barakeh is a Berlin-based conceptual artist and cultural activist. He graduated from the Faculty of Fine Arts in Damascus, Syria in 2005, completed his MFA at Funen Art Academy in Odense, and a Meisterschuler study at the Städelschule Art Academy in Frankfurt. Driven by his observations of longstanding social injustice, Barakeh approaches creative practice as a tool for societal change; manipulating commonplace visual and cultural touchstones to expose and undermine stagnant power structures. In a recent major shift in his work, he has developed a suite of social initiatives that leverage artistic thinking to directly address the issues of contemporary mass migrations. Chief among these projects are the online platform SYRIA Cultural Index, the mobile Syrian Biennale, and the non-profit Coculture e.V. Barakeh has exhibited at Künstlerhaus Stuttgart, The 11th Shanghai Biennale, The Frankfurter Kunstverein, The Busan Biennale, and Museum of Arts and Crafts Hamburg, among many others.

On the Ropes (2015–ongoing)

installation, video
Dimensions: variable, Duration: each video 10 minutes

First Musical Performance: Markus Oeffinger (guitarist, Germany).
Second Performance: Takahashi Marie (violinist, Japan), Aki Kitajima (cellist, Japan),
Marco Ramaglia (pianist, Italy).

Video link: https://vimeo.com/376229542

> *Forms of modern life may differ in quite a few respects—but what unites them all is precisely their fragility, temporariness, vulnerability and inclination to constant change. To 'be modern' means to modernize—compulsively, obsessively; not so much just 'to be', let alone to keep its identity intact, but forever 'becoming', avoiding completion, staying under defined. (...) 'Liquid modernity' is the growing conviction that change is the only permanence, and uncertainty the only certainty.*

—Zygmunt Bauman

On the Ropes underscores a significant moment of permeability between the experience of the immigrant, the artist, and the general citizen of contemporaneity. As humanity progresses deeper into Bauman's "Liquid Modernity", the circumstances of the displaced and the circumstances of the economically and ideologically marginalized cultural producer become more indistinguishable from universal circumstances. Augmenting a reality rife with anxiety and instability, Barakeh suspended every object in his studio-cum-apartment 15 centimeters above the floor on monofilament wire. In a concert entitled *Sounds Like Precarity*, musicians were invited to improvise, compose and play a piece on the wires. An ongoing work that has been shown in Frankfurt, Berlin and Paris to date, each new iteration is a reenactment of the original studio apartment that is staged, filmed and incorporated into subsequent installations and videos.

(Bauman, Zygmunt. *Liquid Modernity.* Polity Press, 2000, p. viii.)

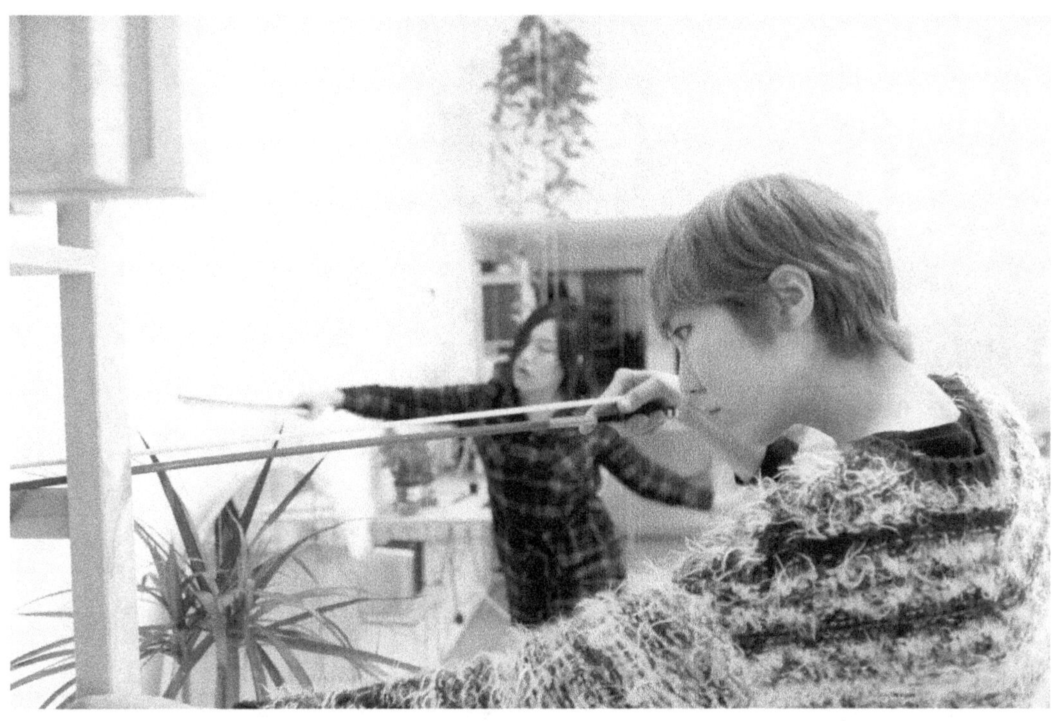

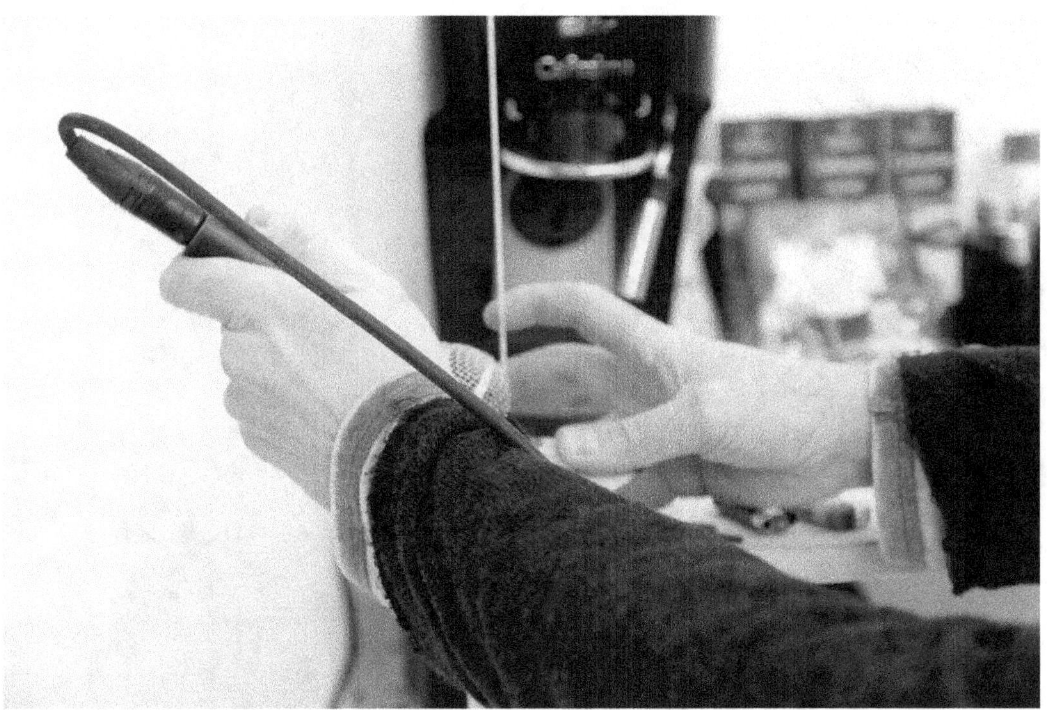

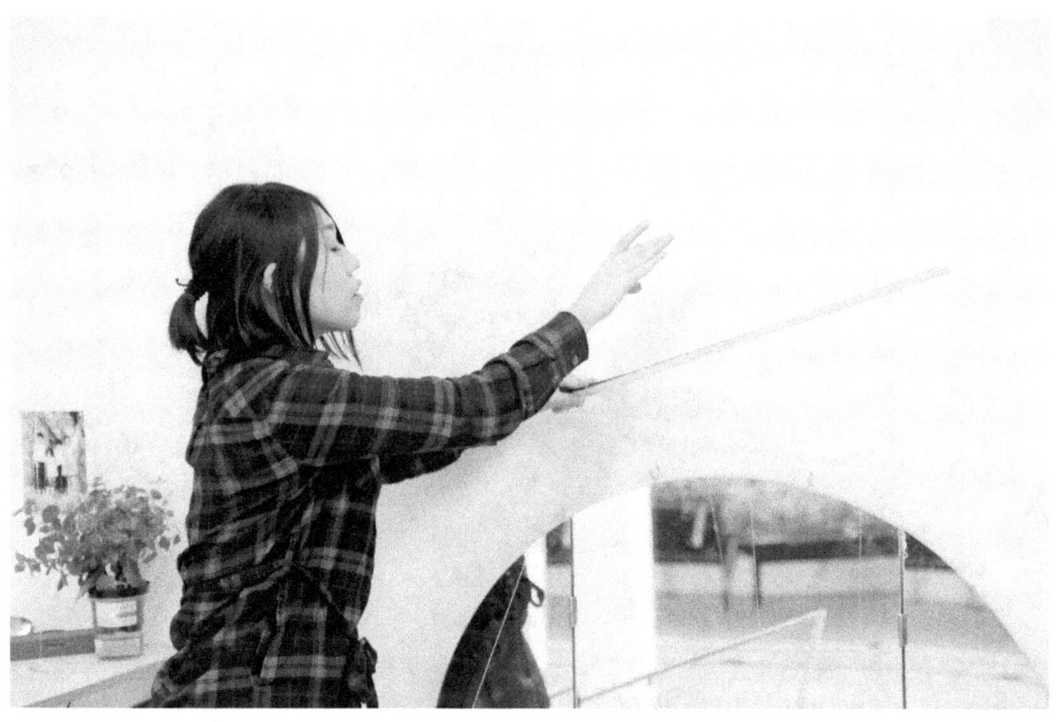

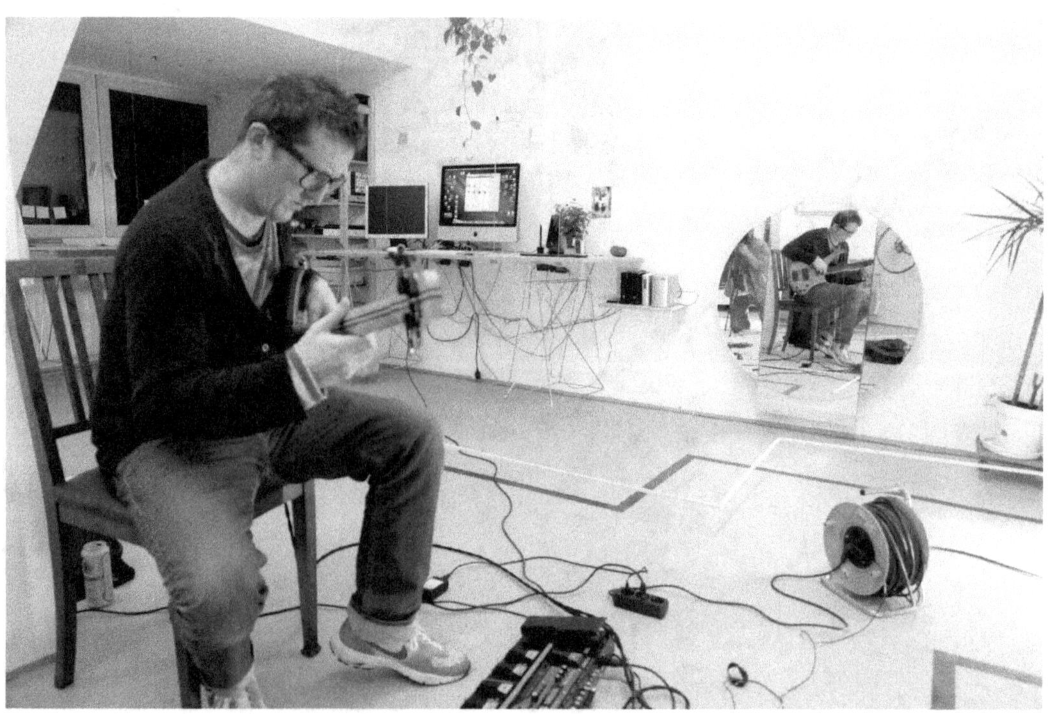

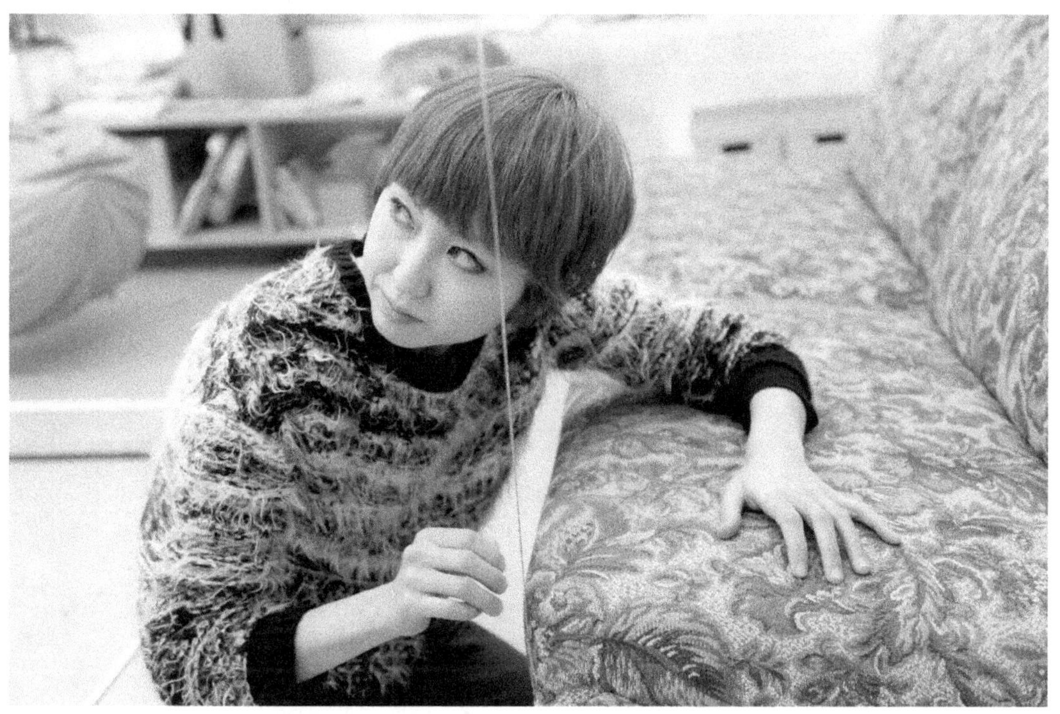

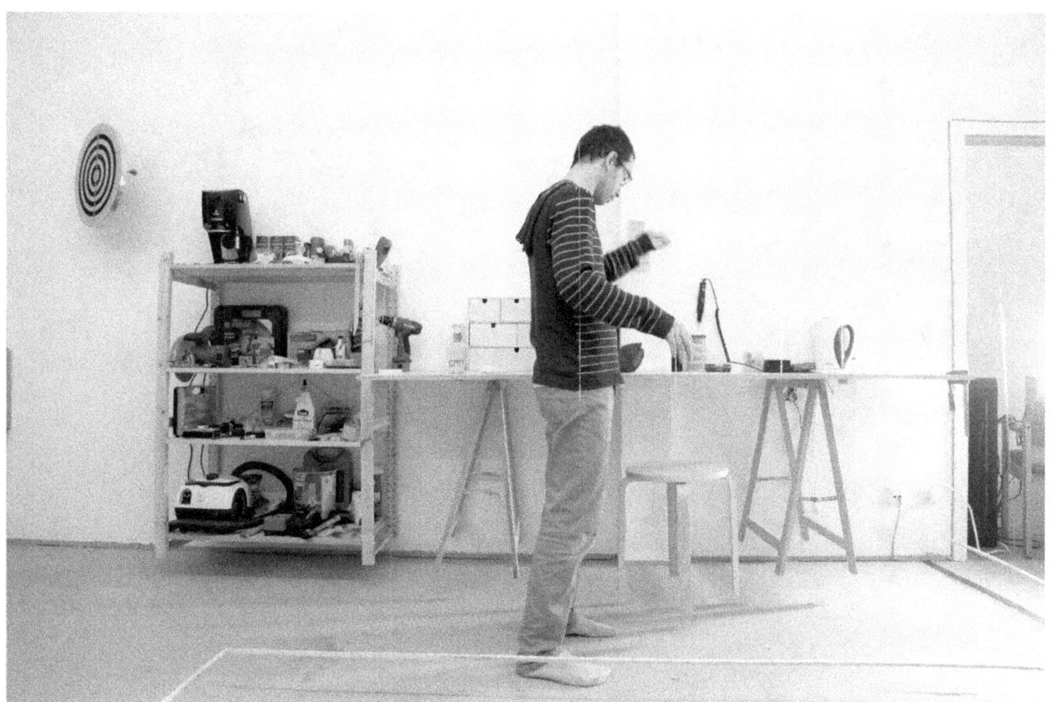

This publication is available open access at:
http://www.ipsonet.org/publications/open-access

Thanks to the generosity of the American Public University System

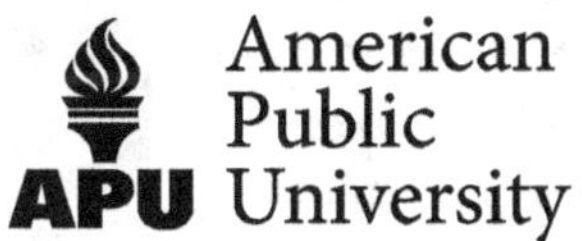 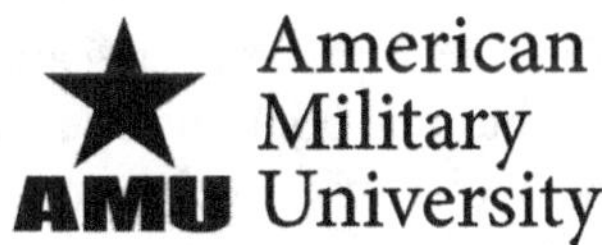

Featured Titles from Westphalia Press

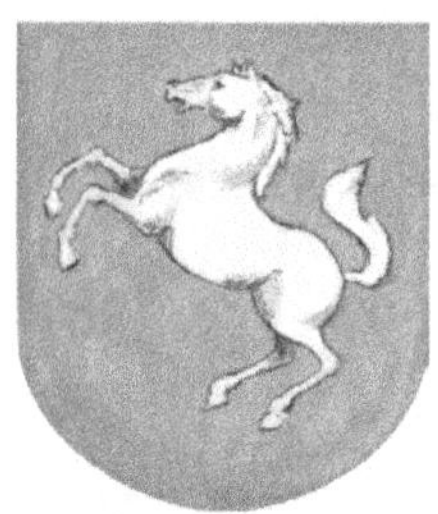

Issues in Maritime Cyber Security Edited by Nicole K. Drumhiller, Fred S. Roberts, Joseph DiRenzo III and Fred S. Roberts

While there is literature about the maritime transportation system, and about cyber security, to date there is very little literature on this converging area. This pioneering book is beneficial to a variety of audiences looking at risk analysis, national security, cyber threats, or maritime policy.

The Death Penalty in the Caribbean: Perspectives from the Police Edited by Wendell C. Wallace PhD

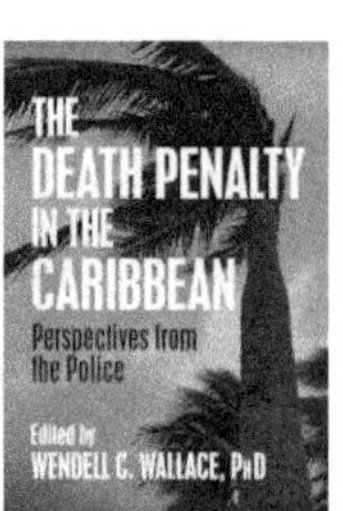

Two controversial topics, policing and the death penalty, are skillfully interwoven into one book in order to respond to this lacuna in the region. The book carries you through a disparate range of emotions, thoughts, frustrations, successes and views as espoused by police leaders throughout the Caribbean

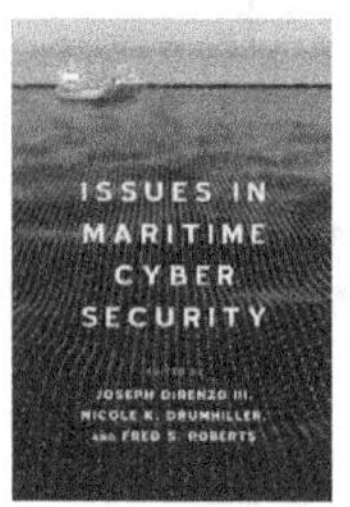

Middle East Reviews: Second Edition
Edited by Mohammed M. Aman PhD and Mary Jo Aman MLIS

The book brings together reviews of books published on the Middle East and North Africa. It is a valuable addition to Middle East literature, and will provide an informative read for experts and non-experts on the MENA countries.

Unworkable Conservatism: Small Government, Freemarkets, and Impracticality by Max J. Skidmore

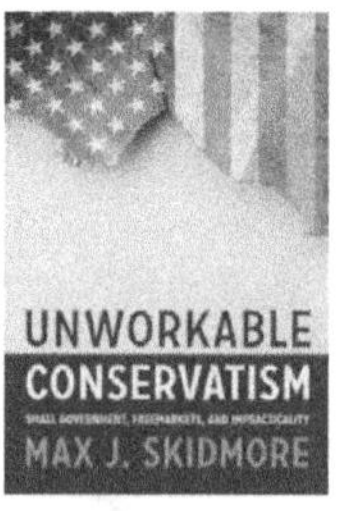

Unworkable Conservatism looks at what passes these days for "conservative" principles—small government, low taxes, minimal regulation—and demonstrates that they are not feasible under modern conditions.

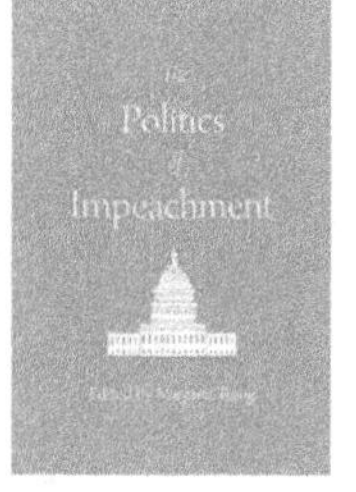

The Politics of Impeachment
Edited by Margaret Tseng

This edited volume addresses the increased political nature of impeachment. It is meant to be a wide overview of impeachment on the federal and state level, including: the politics of bringing impeachment articles forward, the politicized impeachment proceedings, the political nature of how one conducts oneself during the proceedings and the political fallout afterwards.

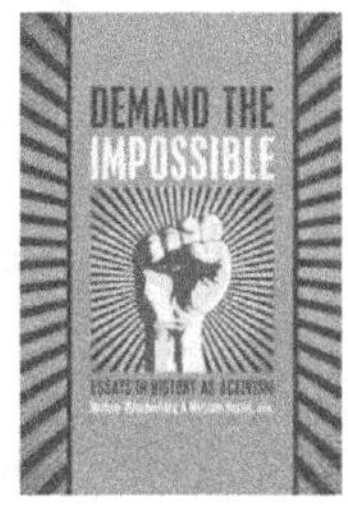

Demand the Impossible: Essays in History as Activism
Edited by Nathan Wuertenberg and William Horne

Demand the Impossible asks scholars what they can do to help solve present-day crises. The twelve essays in this volume draw inspiration from present-day activists. They examine the role of history in shaping ongoing debates over monuments, racism, clean energy, health care, poverty, and the Democratic Party.

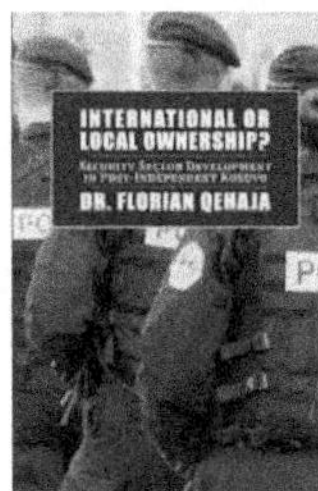

International or Local Ownership?: Security Sector Development in Post-Independent Kosovo by Dr. Florian Qehaja

International or Local Ownership? contributes to the debate on the concept of local ownership in post-conflict settings, and discussions on international relations, peacebuilding, security and development studies.

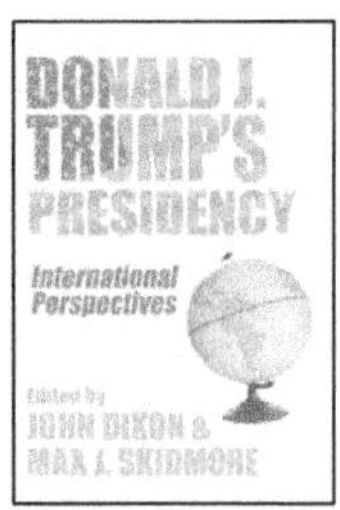

Donald J. Trump's Presidency: International Perspectives
Edited by John Dixon and Max J. Skidmore

President Donald J. Trump's foreign policy rhetoric and actions become more understandable by reference to his personality traits, his worldview, and his view of the world. As such, his foreign policy emphasis was on American isolationism and economic nationalism.

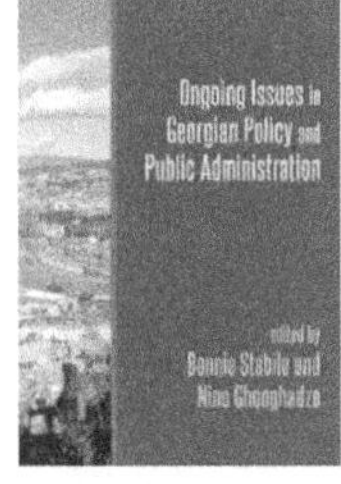

Ongoing Issues in Georgian Policy and Public Administration
Edited by Bonnie Stabile and Nino Ghonghadze

Thriving democracy and representative government depend upon a well functioning civil service, rich civic life and economic success. Georgia has been considered a top performer among countries in South Eastern Europe seeking to establish themselves in the post-Soviet era.

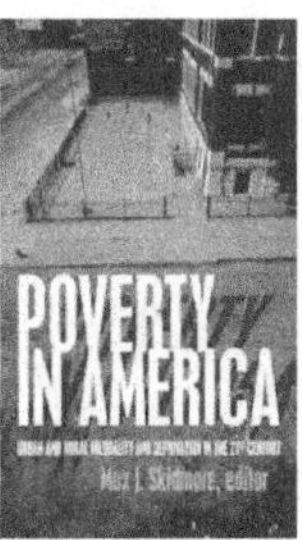

Poverty in America: Urban and Rural Inequality and
Deprivation in the 21st Century
Edited by Max J. Skidmore

Poverty in America too often goes unnoticed, and disregarded. This perhaps results from America's general level of prosperity along with a fairly widespread notion that conditions inevitably are better in the USA than elsewhere. Political rhetoric frequently enforces such an erroneous notion.

westphaliapress.org